The God Pumpers

The God Pumpers
Religion in the Electronic Age

Edited by
Marshall Fishwick
Ray B. Browne

Bowling Green State University Popular Press
Bowling Green, Ohio 43403

CONTENTS

Preface

If the God Pumpers have God Fathers, Oral Roberts is surely one of them. For two generations he has canvassed the land, by tent, auditorium, radio, television. In 1954 his "old time" television set a new style. Twelve years later he left the air, worked out a new "cooler" variety show format, and produced a 1970 Thanksgiving Special that reached 27 million viewers. With him, televangelism came of age.

But there was more. In 1987 he announced that God had appeared and told him he would "take Oral home" if he failed to raise another eight million dollars for his financially-troubled City of Faith in Tulsa. Celestial blackmail! Even some of Oral's staunch admirers gasped at the implications—pay up or drop dead. Some stations even refused to carry future programs that used this tactic. Once again, Oral was exploring new turf.

So was Pat Robertson, who announced that he would not run for the office of President of the United States in 1988 unless three million people petitioned him to do so, and save the Republic. A few years earlier this might have seemed like a regional joke; but by 1987 it was national news, with major newspapers, magazines, and talk shows featuring it. The Iran arms scandal greatly aided his case—the godless would lead us to ruin. For the first time in history two ordained hell-fire preachers—Jesse Jackson and Pat Robertson—were seen as major stars in the political heaven, power brokers who might even sway elections.

Other once-obscure televangelists came center stage. *Newsweek* carried a long story on Jim and Tammy Baker's Heritage, USA, a 2,300 acres Christian theme park just south of Charlotte, N.C., which intended to be a Disneyland for the Devout. In centuries past Christian pilgrims had headed for Canterbury or Lourdes; but today's Bible-hugging Christians choose Heritage USA, with family entertainment courtesy of the Holy Spirit. There are baptisms every Tuesday in the hotel swimming pool; a high-tech Passion play in the amphitheater; and (for night owls) a 2 a.m. daily wafers-and-grapejuice communion service. There is also a water park featuring the world's largest wave pool and a 52-foot water slide that sends Christians careering at 40 mph. And there was more: a full-scale flaming scandal, complete with adultery, wife-swapping, corruption, and blackmail. Televangelism jumped off the religious channels into prime time news. The fires are still raging as we put this book together in the summer of 1987.

1

There was other startling news to welcome in 1987. "Murph the Surf" came out. After 21 years in prison, the famous criminal who stole the Star of India sapphire from the Museum of Natural History, then got two life sentences for murder, was released to the street.

More accurately, to the pulpit. Murph told reporters he planned to be a preacher, doing a caper for Christ. To warm up, he would hit the college lecture circuit, starting at $2,500 an appearance. He did not say whether or not his model was Chuck Colson, Watergate criminal who became a Christian celebrity and best-selling author. But Murph did comment on his own past. "It's like an old movie that we saw years and years ago. It doesn't seem real, doesn't seem like anybody I really knew."

Nor did the steady growth of fundamentalism on college and university campuses (many long identified with secularism and liberalism) seem real to those of us who have spent our lives in academia. Like the resurgent conservatives in national politics, these college crusaders are well organized, well funded, and masters of new technologies. A recent example is a group called CAUSA USA—The Confederation of the Associations for the Unity of the Societies of the Americas. Appearing simultaneously on scores of campuses (including mine), CAUSA asks signers to "agree" there should be a God-centered morality in the U.S., that all people should be free and that communism is dangerous. CAUSA President Joseph Sanchez claimed that over eight million people had signed by March, 1987. At the same time Ronald Hilton, professor emeritus at Stanford University and editor of *World Affairs Report* said that CAUSA is a recruiting front for the Unification Church and the Rev. Sun Myung Moon. Another highly motivated recruiting group called CARP (Collegiate Association for the Research of Principles) makes no secret of its ties to Moon's Unification Church, and has assisted CAUSA.

Whatever CAUSA's ultimate ties, it is clear that Moon has a complex network of organizations world wide, arranging and staging conferences including leading scholars (again, including some from my university). Moon's ties, Professor Hilton said in a widely quoted news release, "have reached a degree of intellectual respectability that is quite surprising."

That same week the *Wall Street Journal* carried a three-column story with this headline: "Fundamentalist Christians Strive to Apply Beliefs to the Workplace." It told of a new Bible-based approach to personal finance, called "Christianomics," of Christian Yellow Pages in phone books, and of an ever-increasing number of companies which blend work and worship. Special attention was paid to Jim Hodges, founder of Hard

Hats for Christ, which ministers to itinerant construction workers. "It used to be that you had to crawl up in a corner to have a Bible study," Hodges was quoted as saying. "Now there are some jobs where you have to attend a study to be a part of the in group."

Clearly media, religion, and popular culture are converging to form a sort of new trinity. No one can say for sure what this means. Like many aspects of popular concern, this union has often been ignored or ridiculed by the elite. Most historians, media critics, and theologians have ignored this new beast, shuffling towards Bethlehem to be born.

We choose not to ignore it. We hope these essays—a series of probes— will engender new interest and research. And we know this is a vital and controversial new addition to American life as the Reagan Era comes to an end.

Marshall Fishwick

From Sea To Shining Sea

Marshall Fishwick

"God, guns, guts—they made America."

Bumper Sticker

"My specific calling from God is to be a TV talk-show host."

Jim Bakker

Picture this: a segment of the Heavenly City, the New Jerusalem, in beautiful Garden Grove, California, translucent and iridescent, with sunlight coming through 10,000 windows of tempered silver colored glass, held in place by a lace-like frame of white trusses. The ninety foot doors are open, beckoning us in. Fountains shoot jets of water heavenward, and music from one of the world's largest pipe organs fills the air.

This is the Crystal Palace, dedicated "To the Glory of Man For the Greater Glory of God," where thousands have come to celebrate the birthday of the Greatest Nation on Earth. Huge white concrete columns, the largest ever poured, hold balconies in place. Amidst the flowing fountains and exotic plants are an array of American flags. Up front are grand military bands, in full dress uniform. They play patriotic songs; feet tap to the drum beat, television cameras pan in and out, catching smiles, hugs, sliding trombones. This is indeed a Glorious Fourth.

Out strides the Preacher, in robes as blue as the California sky. Eyes twinkling, teeth glistening, he speaks words that are his trade-mark: "This is the day the Lord hath made..." This is the day, all those seated in church (or in the drive-in sanctuary) well know: Robert Schuller will deliver "I am the American Flag:" the sermon which won the Principal Award from the Freedoms Foundation and has since become a "tradition"

4

Robert Schuller: accent the positive.

on patriotic occasions. Pop goes the Preacher, adopting the person of the flag, using exaggerated gestures and expressions. "I, the flag, have seen much," he intones. "So listen and listen hard."[1]

Starting with the blood and snow of Valley Forge, he takes us to Pork Chop Hill, Verdun, Normandy, Iwo Jima, and the Asian jungles. On we go to Brownie, Cub Scout and Boy Scout meetings, to Little Leagues, Pony Leagues, Minor and Major Leagues. "Dream your dreams! Dare to believe! You can make it in America!" With a steady rising crescendo of sound, Schuller reaffirms the greatness of God and the American Way of Life. "I dream of new airports, new doors opening, old walls falling and old ideologies fading away.... We stand today on the threshold of a new day, a new era, a new age. Rise up and make your country and your world great!"[2]

Out go his arms in a grand gesture—perhaps like Christ's to the multitudes on the Mount. Bands blare. Lines of flags are borne by smartly-uniformed youths marching down the aisles. Suddenly a gigantic American flag descends, stretching from ceiling to floor. People gasp, gurgle, clap. Super-flag in super-church! It even covers and conceals the altar. Never mind, we can still see Robert Schuller; and he *is* both the preacher and the American flag.

No less dramatic is the Rev. Terry Cole-Whittaker in nearby La Jolla, California. Reminiscent of a young Dinah Shore, blonde, trim, and throaty, she belts out her theme song: "I Gotta Be Me." While preaching she plays her audience like a Carol Burnett or a Joan Rivers— puns, pokes, and gags; quips instead of answers:

"People want to know what my stand on abortion is." Pause, suspense, punch line: "I think the Pope should have the choice of whether he wants an abortion or not!" Laughs, jeers, roars. "I want that man to have everything he wants, bless him." On to the next topic.[3]

She prays that we be released from all guilt having to do with sexuality, money, power. "God *loves* you" is her standard refrain line. "He never judged or condemned you." The Inquisition might well have burned her. California crowds pitch big bucks into the collection plate, and rush back for more. Her TV sign-off is "I love you."

The Rev. Terry doesn't fit the role of the liberated feminist: she has no quarrel with the male-dominated church and its patriarchal ways. What she has—and is ready to exploit —is sex appeal. She claims to be monogamous, though serially. Wed and divorced four times, breaking off a recent "close relationship" with a staff member, Terry has yet to equal her great-grandmother's record of six marriages. That venerable lady, a spokesman for Religious Science, passed strong beliefs down through the generations; not only Terry but all three of her sisters are ministers adhering to Christian fundamentalism. Going from Newport Harbor High School (where she says she did the "dumb blonde act"), Terry attended Orange Coast College where she was homecoming queen. Married but not graduated, she became Mrs. California in 1968, then runner-up to the runner-up for Mrs. America. Two divorces later (in 1975) she studied at the Ernest Holmes School of Ministry, became the minister at the La Jolla Church of Religious Science, and married an ex-professional football player. Then in 1982 she divorced the husband and the church, explaining: "I couldn't be limited by an organization. I had to be part of something that could change instantly."

One thing she did was put big bucks into television. Her half-hour show (part preaching, part studio-audience therapy) appears in 15 markets, including New York City, Los Angeles and San Francisco. The congregation, by *Wall Street Journal* estimate,　ran up a $10 million annual budget. Cole-Whittaker herself was paid $180,000 in salary in 1984 exclusive of book profits. Not yet in the big league, but coming up fast.

"I tell people what they want to hear," candidly admits Cole-Whittaker. "Who wouldn't want to know how beautiful they are?" Norman Vincent Peale has been selling positive thinking since the Depression—but never with such glitz and intimacy and sex appeal.

Though churches and cults ripen like lemons in the California sun, none has yet equalled that Old Master of Healing—and Appealing—Oral Roberts. His headquarters is in oil-rich Tulsa, Oklahoma. There he has built, over 40 years, a half-billion dollar evangelical, educational and medical center.[4] Here in the City of Faith (supported by over $6 million a month from prayer partners) is Oral Roberts University, dedicated to "Christian virtue in academics and athletics." Nearby is the towering 60-story medical and research center, where patients' spiritual needs are as carefully attended to as their physical needs. How was such a structure financed?

In his 1980 fund-raising letter, Oral Roberts told of his vision. A 900-foot Jesus had urged him to go for 60 stories. A few years later Jesus came again—to let him know that if each prayer partner sent in $240, a supernatural cancer-cure breakthrough would occur in the Tower of Faith. Where did the actual vision come? "I went to the desert," Brother Oral replied.

But his former daughter-in-law (who divorced Oral's son Richard in 1979) added a caustic footnote. "When he said 'I went to the desert,'" she told the press, "he meant he went to the Palm Desert playing golf. When God talks to Oral it's in very convenient terms for his next corporate moves."

Oral and son Richard were undaunted. While Oral spoke from his auditorium in Tulsa, Richard (dressed in African robes) spoke via satellite from Nigeria. The program, billed as "the greatest healing service since the day of the apostles," was beamed to large-screen TV screens in hundreds of churches, rented auditoriums, hotel ballrooms and theaters in 211 U.S. and Canadian cities. The news from Nigeria was good. "Growths and tumors and cancers have been healed, and thousands have accepted Jesus," Richard told his world-wide audience. If the money were forthcoming, Oral added, healing teams from his university would go out "across America and all the world." Quite a program for a dirt-poor farm boy who enrolled at Oklahoma Baptist University in 1943, never graduated, and doesn't hold any earned degree.

Like many pop evangelists, Oral is grooming son Richard to take over, but competition gets tougher year by year. The East Coast has got into the act; some of the brightest, most inventive pumpers are there. One—Jerry Falwell—has become the national symbol of the New Right and the Moral Majority. He is being linked to Ronald Reagan as Billy Graham was once linked to Dwight D. Eisenhower; Falwell's giving the final benediction at the 1984 Republican Convention strengthened that connection.

In 1956, Falwell, this young graduate of a Baptist Seminary, founded the Thomas Road Baptist Church in Lynchburg, Virginia, with 35 members. They bought an old soft drink bottling plant. Jerry recalls they started by "getting the syrup off the floor." (Some say he's been bottling it with a new holy label ever since.) A few weeks later he launched his "Old Time Gospel Hour" on a local radio station, then on television. Money and members poured in. In the midst of the Baptist belt, Falwell had hit a warm, responsive cord. By 1970 there were over 10,000 church members, and a new octagonal church with a Thomas Jefferson classical design. When that number doubled in a few years, Falwell thrust himself on the national scene. He bought "Treasure Island" to let young Christians vacation and pray; took in unwed mothers to stem the tide of abortion; started his own college (Liberty Baptist), beginning modestly with old buildings, then buying a 4,000 acre tract for a modern university with thousands of students. The students flock in as new buildings rise.

But Falwell's master stroke, nationally speaking, was to found the Moral Majority in 1979, as a private citizen determined to return the wayward nation to "old time morality," and foil Communists, homosexuals, abortionists, radicals, street demonstrators, and other "enemies." He found a specific devil in Larry Flynt, editor of *Hustler*, who pictured Falwell in pseudo "lickker ads," and accused him of having had his first sex with his Mother. Using these taunts with great skill and bringing a highly-publicized law suit against Flynt, Falwell pushed forward, gathering an army of preachers as co-workers. By 1983, he had representatives in 65 foreign nations (mostly in refugee camps) and an estimated six million television viewers across America. No one knew how many more watched in Canada, Africa, and Japan—nor how many tuned in to the radio show.[5]

That bastion of Establishment respectability, *The Wall Street Journal*, was impressed. A man of "charm, talent, drive and ambition," Falwell—based in this traditional city in Piedmont, Virginia—had created "the fastest growing of any of the big time religious programs," using the same tactics of corporations and conglomerates that made Wall Street itself function. Whatever help the Lord rendered, Falwell himself used modern marketing and management techniques with great skill. He knew how to administer, admonish, and advertise; and, *The Wall Street Journal* reporter added, in terms his readers could understand, Falwell had "a keen understanding of income statements and balance sheets."[6] We shall draw up our own balance sheet on Falwell in a later chapter. In claiming to speak for the Moral Majority, Jerry Falwell became not merely the dynamic pastor of a Baptist Church, but the head of a popular national movement. In the first national debate between Ronald Reagan and Walter Mondale, on October 7, 1984, the Democratic challenger went so far as to suggest that Falwell would dictate appointments to the Supreme Court were Reagan re-elected.

Preachers and politics have formed new alliances—the Moral Majority is widely credited with facilitating conservative victories at the polls in 1980, 1982, and 1984. Politicians go to church, cameras follow. Senator Ted Kennedy confronts Jerry Falwell on his home turf—Liberty Baptist College. The media decide that the right label is "Daniel in the Lion's Den." If not much blood was spilled, Biblical quotations are strewn all over the landscape. Both sides up their media ratings. Who says religion isn't entertainment?

Certainly not Pat Robertson and Jim Bakker, two rivals who have grown up in Falwell Country—one to the east in Virginia Beach, the other to the south, in Charlotte. Pat Robertson, perhaps the best educated

God pumper, is the son of a former United States Senator, Willis Robertson. His Virginia Beach Center, home of the $500 million Christian Broadcasting Network (CBN), includes four television stations, a recording company, a 24-hour-a-day programming service available to more than 3,000 cable systems, a news network, university, and satellite earth station. Raised in a small Virginia town, graduated from the University of Virginia and Yale Law School, Pat Robertson was frustrated when he failed to pass the bar exams. After a short period of social work in the Brooklyn slums, he purchased a defunct Virginia Beach television station in 1960, and went on the air in 1961.

His centerpiece is the "700 Club," a Christian type of Johnny Carson's "Tonight Show," complete with sophisticated camera crews, stage props, and skyline backdrop. Why 700? Robertson began in 1965 using the telethon and telephone volunteers with the goal of getting 700 people to pledge ten dollars a month. And lo, the hundreds did become thousands. Here "celebrity meets celebrity," as Robertson interviews fascinating people who write best sellers, lead the Hit Parade, roam the Corridors of Power. They all have one common denominator: they are born-again Christians, who make their pitch, and thus bolster CBN. The whole thing worked so well that Jim Bakker left to begin the PTL (Praise the Lord) Club in 1974 in Charlotte, North Carolina. By 1978 it appeared on over 200 stations nation-wide—more affiliates than the entire ABC network.

But like youthful Alexander the Great, Jim yearned for other kingdoms to conquer. Heady with the success of PTL ("Praise the Lord"— or as a naughty critic suggested, "Pass the Loot?"), he bought a vast tract of land, and set out to build the first Christian theme-park, to serve as headquarters for his world-wide evangelism and electronic campaigns. With the omni-present wife Tammy and children Tammy Sue and Jamie Charles, he is constructing a vast multi-million dollar "Twenty First Century Fellowship Center" with a Grand Hotel featuring "turn of the century elegance." (The contradiction of entering the next century by reverting to the style of the last is a hallmark of contemporary evangelism). The park is obviously modeled on Disney World, further down the road in Florida. There is a cutesy-folksy Main Street (as the brochure puts it, "a delightful, old fashioned potpourri of quaint shops and cafes, all beneath a soaring climate-controlled cyclorama ceiling that creates its own weather moods"), a Grand Palace Cafeteria ("the largest cafeteria of its kind"), and a Seminar/Conference Center (home of PTL's Total Learning Center Workshops, and the great Hall of Agreement), and Heritage Grand Towers.

Pat Robertson, 1988 candidate for the White House.

Pat & Dede at work in studio A at CBN headquarters.

But neither the Towers nor the PTL looked grand when Jim Bakker admitted he had been guilty of adultery with a church secretary; and that blackmail had been involved. Turning his ministry over to Jerry Falwell, Bakker was defrocked, and evidence of scandal and corruption set the media aglow. The fall-out affected other ministries as well. In June, 1987 the Rev. Pat Robertson announced 500 layoffs at the Christian Broadcasting Network noting that a recent Gallup poll had shown that half of all donors to religious radio and televisoin programs had stopped giving.

Yet no one can doubt that preachers like Robert Schuller, Jerry Falwell, Pat Robertson, and Oral Roberts have become power-brokers of the first magnitude. The new religious spirit cuts across classes, creeds, city and country; it is endemic. Of all the places I found it, the one that intrigues me most is a thriving church nestled between two giant neon Exxon signs in the fashionable Washington suburb of Roslyn, Virginia. Here, in the church locals call Our Lady of Exxon, both the idea and title of this book were born.

Pumping is the order of the day. While service station attendants pump gas, Preacher Jim Robertson pumps God and is not apologetic. "I say if they can pump as much downstairs as we do upstairs, they're doing good!" Here, at least, Christ and culture are compatible.

There are some sticky moments. One occurred recently at a wedding. Preacher reached the "Speak now or forever hold your peace" line just as the Exxon mechanic revved up a 3,000 horsepower race car. Quick negotiations followed. The mechanic stopped until the wedding finished. Everyone agreed that the newly-weds and the newly-tuned car got off to good starts.

God pumping takes on the guise of a new gold rush. Selling Salvation is one of the Seven Lively Arts. Pop music has become a major component. Pop singers with cuddly names like Debbie (Boone) and Evie (Tornquest) vie with preachers for popularity—especially with college youth.[7] Roman Catholicism has met new challenges. Not only Pope John Paul II, but the Christ he represents, have become super stars. Protestant preachers with friendly names like Jerry, Jim, Pat, Oral, and Terry have become household words. No nickel-and-dimers these; they go after and get millions. Instead of tents, they preach in Crystal Palaces, market records and talking Bibles, found universities, and start medical schools. The Lord blesses them Real Good.

Are we in the midst of a new and unexpected Turn to the Right— a "back to basics" in religion that parallels what is going on in politics, economics, and education?[7] Was the "Death of God" (like that of Mark

The Holy Father as TV celebrity.

The power of music, and the joy of certainty.

Fundamentalism wears many faces. The cross functions as symbol on many levels. This is the K.K.K.

Twain) greatly exaggerated? Perhaps, but historians urge caution. They remind us that what was widely heralded as the Great Revival of the 1950's turned out to be the upswing of a roller coaster that later plummeted. Many still recall the over-investment in buildings, seminaries, camps, and missions. By the mid-1960's two major mainline churches, the Episcopal and Presbyterian, had lost more than half a million members. The dilemma was summed up in the title of Carl S. Dudley's book: *Where Have All Our People Gone?*

Many went to the fundamentalist and evangelical churches—even more to the T.V. set to watch televangelists. Surveys in the early 1980's indicated that one out of every four American adults claimed to be an Evangelical (a term which is hard to define and delimit). Religion had become a growth industry. Church membership in the United States is growing twice as fast as the population.[8]

What does all this mean? Have we been caught up in a genuine Great Awakening, matching or surpassing three earlier ones in the 18th, 19th, and early 20th century? What role are new electronic media playing? Will a high tech society turn to mass mediated religions? Must the traditional churches alter their approaches, appeals, and structures to survive?

Are some televangelists selling indulgences, prayers, trinkets, records, even miracles? In order to pay for the new electronic complexes, they are not only proclaiming but marketing. Jim Bakker makes no bones about it: "We have a better product than soap or automobiles. We have eternal life." "If Jesus were on earth today," says Jimmy Swaggert, "he'd be on TV."

And what do we—the American public—have: a revival or a rip-off? That is our central question.

The question is simple, but the answer is complex and conflicting. To get a dogmatic or definitive answer one must look elsewhere. Religion in America is (among other things) diffuse, fragmented, and internalized.[9] Instead of being confined to churches, it spills out all over the land— in sports events, festivals, fairs, civil ceremonies, and beauty contests ranging from Miss World to Miss Onion Queen of Jones County. One can be inundated with "religious" stimuli and talk without going near a church or synagogue. Efforts to transform, improve, release, or rejuvenate "the self" have reached epic proportions. When "official" religion doesn't meet ordinary people's needs, or when social confusion reaches the point where institutional patterns can't explain them, new variants appear; new blossoms sprout on the trees.[10]

So we must look at the roots and blossoms of American religion, having suggested a few of the definitions and categories which make meaningful God Talk possible. The questions we ask today have been asked for four centuries on our shores—and for countless centuries elsewhere. Our past will be our prologue. Only when we know something of yesterday's God pumpers can we judge today's.

** ** **

But where does "yesterday" begin when one attempts to understand God and those who proclaim Him? It goes back to times when history was blind, and no record was made. Creation myths exist in every culture; folklore blends with liturgy and ritual. We may have started a new nation, but we inherited a very old religion. Our religious roots, as white colonists, are in Europe, where history and time set religion's boundaries. In America, space set the boundaries. Engulfed and overwhelmed by endless empty land, we seemed adrift in limitless and holy space, free from the burden of history. But we never forgot the Judeo-Christian tradition, perpetuated by conscious constant effort, the chief cornerstone of American life.

This core, alive today, has been transmitted from generation to generation, affirmed by churches, sects, and cults; nourished by reading and re-reading a standard body of literature whose metaphors, parables, and forms of thought saturated our culture.

In ancient times God made a covenant with Israel; in modern times, with America. In both places, the "Chosen People" idea was crucial. The holy shadow of Jehovah—fierce, jealous, paternal—is still cast over our land.

In ancient Israel, only one man—the High Priest—could say God's name and then only one day a year, in the Holy of Holies. To blaspheme God, and utter His name, was a heinous crime—violating the Ten Commandments.

The pendulum swings, customs crumble. Jesus, the Christian God, is on Broadway a Superstar. His name echoes around the world, in more tongues than we can count. Media and religion have always worked together. Before man had an alphabet, he painted, chiseled, and molded god-like images and icons. He built pyramids, tombs, and temples to honor and house the gods. Later on, he wrote of them: the word Bible is derived from a Greek word (*biblion*) which means book. The first book Gutenberg published was the Bible; and one of the greatest benefactors from the new printing press was Martin Luther. Should we not expect that the electronic media are quickly, widely, and effectively adapted to God talk?

That new media have revolutionized our culture is a truism. To the year's four seasons we have introduced a fifth—the television season, which stays with us throughout the other four. The world is (or soon will be) wired for sight and sound. But what about understanding?

Of the airing of religious programs, and the writing of religious books, there is no end. Once no one dared speak of God: now many seem to speak of nothing else. Religious solicitations fill our channels and mail boxes, religious books our bookstores. The hills are alive with preaching. Columns about religion compete with Art Buchwald and Erma Bombeck in newspapers. Free religious magazines clutter airports and dentists' offices. Broadcasters beam out a non-stop warning about hell and Antichrist (who is even now trying to get their program off the air—help!). Television features hard-sell specialists who push not soap but salvation. The cleverest have not only moved over into prime time, they have even got their own channels and networks. Praise the Lord!

Meanwhile, sects and cults have been too busy telling their own stories to examine the larger world in which we live. Bigtime Pop Preachers are so intent on selling their wares that they are ignoring the consequences of god huckstering. Key words and definitions have become meaningless. Just who are liberal secular humanists, evangelicals, fundamentalists, charismatics, and neo-evanglists? What do we mean when we say we are "born again?" When asked to "make a decision," just what are you deciding? When and how do "decisions" come from a creative act of the spirit? With all this God talk, who listens? "If the history of religions is to further the rise of a new humanism," Mircea Eliade writes, "the historian must bring out the autonomous value— the value of a spiritual creation." In the academy, theologians must deal not only with Christianity, but also comparative religion, morphology, phenomenology, semiotics, and anthropology. Given all this material, scholars busy themselves with textual analysis, authorship, the "Q" problem, dating and authenticating. Who does this affect—and how? Is Academia "out of touch?"

We hope not. This book is an effort to show how popular culture, popular preaching, and contemporary function, blend, and alter our lives. What can we say of religion as we near the end of the twentieth century?

Notes

[1]When one writes the Crystal Cathedral for Schuller's text, he gets the sermon, color photographs, and "a press kit that hopefully will help to answer your questions" from the Nason Media Corporation in Anaheim, California—where Disneyland is located. There is a poetic justice in juxtaposition.

[2]Robert Schuller, *I Am The American Flag*, p. 24.

[3]See D. Keith Mano, "Terry Cole-Whittaker," in *People* Magazine, November 26, 1984, pp. 99-103.

[4]Richard Quebedeaux, *By What Authority: The Rise of Personality Cults in American Christianity*, p. 58.

[5]For more on the Falwell story, see Ben Armstrong, *The Electric Church* (Nashville: Nelson, 1979), pp. 115f.

[6]Jim Montgomery, "The Electric Church," in *The Wall Street Journal*, May 19, 1978, p. 15.

[7]See James Gray, "Freshman Veering to Right," in *Berkeley Independent and Gazette*, February 1, 1981, p. 3.

[8]Constant J. Jaquet, editor of *Yearbook of American Churches*, admits that some denominational figures may be "somewhat inflated." When the Church of God in Christ updated its figures in 1982, they went from 425,000 to 3.3 million. The Church of Jesus Christ of Latter-Day Saints picked up an extra 650,000 members by including unbaptized youth. Growth rates of various Pentacostal Holiness churches "raised questions of credibility." Final '82 figures: .9% pop. increase, but 2.7% annual church membership increase.

[9]Peter Williams discusses these terms in his "Introduction" to *Popular Religion in America*. So does Thomas Luckman in *The Invisible Religion* (London, Macmillan, 1970).

[10]Robert N. Bellah, "Civil Religion in America," in William G. McLoughlin and Robert N. Bellah, eds., *Religion in America* (Boston: Beacon, 1968).

Lost Dogs and Financial Healing: Deconstructing Televangelist Miracles

Gary McCarron

Even the slightest trace of piety in us ought to make us feel that a God who cures a headcold at the right moment or tells us to get into a coach just as a downpour is about to start is so absurd a God he would have to be abolished even if he existed. ·Nietzsche

Hume and Contingency Miracles

In his *Inquiry Concerning Human Understanding* (1748), David Hume advanced an argument against believing in miracles that remains influential today. According to Hume, one can only accept an event as a miracle if the likelihood of the event proving true is greater than the likelihood of the claimant's account proving false. In other words, if it is more likely that the claimant is lying, deceived, deluded, or mistaken than it is that the laws of nature have been violated, one has good cause for rejecting the claim that a given occurrence was a miracle. It is far more likely that a human being will be in error for some undefined reason than that nature would alter its course.

Powerful as Hume's argument has proven, it has not been without its critics (Rao, 1981, e.g.). Moreover, Hume's attack is directed against a specific and traditional notion of the miraculous, namely, supernatural intervention in the normal actions of nature. But not all claims for the miraculous fall into this category. There is one class of miracles, it would appear, against which Hume's argument fares rather poorly.

Many of the events today's televangelists see as miraculous have nothing to do with the notion of nature suddenly deviating from its discernible patterns. More often than not, televangelist miracles involve personal salvation, victories by athletes, successful business plans, financial gains, and reunions with lost pets. And even when they claim miracles for events which appear to be instances of supernatural activity,

19

closer inspection shows those happenings to be well within the realm of natural explanation. Though Pat Robertson of the '700 Club' may regard the prayers of his followers as instrumental in turning back a hurricane from his television headquarters in Virginia Beach, the nation's meteorologists found nothing unusual in the storm's pattern. The same holds true for many alleged cases of medical miracles. Though such cures may be low probability events, they happen because of natural processes in the body successfully battling the affliction. But if a theist chooses to regard that event as a miracle, the critic can offer little in the way of rebuttal.

In the cases of financial gains and sporting victories, there is clearly no place to argue for a reversal or cessation of natural laws. Indeed, these events have not even happened against the weight of overwhelming odds. This is where Hume's argument loses its efficacy, for there is often nothing extraordinary in the event for which the televangelist asserts miraculous intervention. If the Christian athlete claims a miracle in the success of his team, there is no point in putting Hume's formula to the test, for it is *not* more likely that the claimant is lying or in error than it is that the event took place. The critic cannot deny the event once it has happened. Televangelist miracles escape the sting of Hume's critique by simply being so ordinary.

According to Holland (1965), we can distinguish between these two classes of miracles. Miracles in which no law of nature is said to be breached are called contingency miracles. Those miracles in which natural law is transgressed—as in the parting of the Red Sea—are called violation miracles.

Contingency miracles describe events which defy probability or seem too remarkable to explain as coincidences. Violation miracles, on the other hand, describe events unexplainable by the laws of nature. Praying that your tangled parachute will open before it is too late—and then having it do so—is a contingency miracle. Coming to a stop in the midst of your free fall so you can untangle it before continuing earthward is a violation miracle.

Violation miracles are event-oriented: the extraordinary thing about them is the event that is claimed to have happened. Contingency miracles are interpretation-oriented: they are miraculous only because the believer interprets them that way. In the case of violation miracles the critic's most effective tactic is to challenge the claim that the event took place. In the interpretation-oriented nature of contingency miracles, however, matters are somewhat different. That the event took place is rarely denied. The target of the critic's aim here is not the event but the claim that the event was miraculous. In other words, it is the theist's interpretive account that is challenged, an interpretation that turns otherwise commonplace events into claims for miraculous activity.

But challenging an interpretation is a far different thing than challenging a claim that natural laws have been violated by divine forces. Thus the best way to deal with contingency miracles is not to argue that the events in question could not have occurred, but rather to try and understand why those everyday occurrences have been elevated to the status of the miraculous. With the kinds of events that televangelists offer their viewers as miracles, it is actually more profitable for a social and cultural critic to inquire into the choices that are made in deciding which commonplace experiences will be accorded the privilege of being called miracles. For somewhere a choice is made, though it is certainly conceivable that the processes which lead to those choices are far from being conscious deliberations. In what follows, then, I will try to offer a deconstruction of certain televangelist miracles in the hope of revealing some of the underlying rationale that guides the selection process. It is a central contention of this paper that by calling an event "miraculous," televangelists betray significant features of their socio-political philosophy by indicating what sorts of events are symbolically important. Whereas scriptural miracles were signs of God's intentions, televangelist miracles are signs which offer us insights into the conservative ideology that holds the fundamentalist worldview together.

The Miracle of the Lost Dog

During a '700 Club' television broadcast in the summer of 1986, the following testimonial was presented. A born-again family discovered to their dismay that their pet dog had gone missing. They searched everywhere and telephoned neighbours, but could find no trace of the animal. With all natural avenues for the dog's recovery exhausted they turned to supernatural avenues and began to pray.

In due course their prayers were answered, for after a period of a few weeks the dog was found by strangers and returned. In joy they claimed a miracle.

The miracle of the lost dog is a perplexing one for the secular critic, for nothing in the account presented on television suggested the mysterious powers of coincidence or the working of inexplicable forces. The animal's return was a contingency miracle in which the unfolding of events was so commonplace as to make the claim of miraculous intervention seem absurd. But from within the framework that is the fundamentalist world view, the claim was logical indeed. The family was delighted by the return of their pet and regarded the event as a miracle. They did so because their fundamentalist beliefs led them to impose a causal interpretive scheme on what would otherwise be seen as an ordinary experience. Faith transformed the profane into the sacred.

But why a lost dog? The extent to which this miracle validates the Christian sentiment that God cares for all his creatures cannot be overlooked, and that God would deign to look after so helpless an animal is certainly commendable. Yet this miracle portrays God as someone whose priorities seem at odds with the pressing affairs of human life. Kind though he is to return a lost pet, what about the many lost children—figurative and literal—presently wandering the world?

But to perceive the miracle as absurd stems from a failure to recognize the symbolic connotations implied in the event: The dog is the prodigal son returning to his father, the legions of lost innocents reunited with their guardians. Hence the miracle functions as a claim that God will protect the least of us if our lives are bound to his will.

By neutralizing the absurdity of the miracle through analysis, one is still left facing the literal event. The two-fold process of selection—the family's choice to call this event a miracle, and the '700 Club's' decision to air it on television—points to the fact that something important is contained in the account, and however trivial the event may seem, there is no escaping the need to inquire into its symbolic functions.

If this miracle is described as an event in which what is made manifest is God's concern for the most helpless of living beings, one starts to recognize the import of its symbolic connections. Add to this formulation the role of a loving family, and the miracle begins to emerge as a pro-life, pro-family statement. The miracle of the lost dog is thus a claim that all life is sacred, and that the family must play a role in safeguarding that imperative. It is really a narrative in which issues crucial to the fundamentalist ideology are allowed prominent play: pro-life claims opposing abortion; pro-family views challenging ERA. The miracle of the lost dog is a political statement reaffirming the basic moral issues out of which the coalition between fundamentalist faith and conservative politics has been built. It is an attack against those measures which conservatives and fundamentalists alike see as corrupting influences in the American dream.

Deconstructed this way, it is apparent that the crux of the miracle is its life-affirming nature, and the "absurdity" of the God who protects lost dogs is only an interpretation imposed by people who remain outside the fundamentalist world. In one sense, then, the miracle cannot be explained as the event, but must be seen as the relationship between

God, family, and preacher as this takes place within the sphere of fundamentalist thought. The event brings the miracle into being, but is itself only one element in a complicated formula necessary for divine power to be made manifest.

The fundamentalist's world view is given its meaning through the mediating role God plays in the individual relations and actions of each and every member of the faith. As the focal point of all attention, God's will is made synonymous with the unfolding of world history and individual griefs and triumphs. By returning the lost dog to its owner, God is seen by the followers of Pat Robertson as a kindly figure concerned with the welfare of defenseless life, and devoted to the preservation of the American family. The theist delights in the apparent absurdity of this miracle, for it "proves" that if God is willing to spare the life of a dog—though a Christian dog, it should be added—then it is inconceivable that he could be unfeeling about the plight of human sufferers. Hence the miracle of the lost dog is truly what a miracle should be: a sign. It is an event that stands for something other than what it is.

Financial Salvation

A married couple who are members of Pat Robertson's '700 Club' are in financial difficulties. The husband has lost his job, and the wife, true to Christian precepts, cannot take one, for she must stay at home with the children and tend to the house. Their bank account is slowly dwindling. Against what would normally be regarded as commonsense, they write a cheque to the '700 Club' and mail it away, trusting in what Pat Robertson has described in his "Kingdom Principles" as a law of reciprocity by which those who tithe regularly are blessed by God with rewards that exceed the amount of their donation. One week after sending their cheque to CBN, the couple find a cheque in their mailbox for ten-fold what they sent to Pat Robertson. A miracle! Of course, what is frequently passed over in testimonials of this sort is the origin of the second cheque. In virtually all cases it is money that was owed to the recipients and which simply showed up at a fortunate moment. Sometimes, as if to make its appearance even more mysterious, the second cheque will be issued by an agency like the IRS which happens to be making amends for an error committed by their offices some years before. Because the couple recently sent money to CBN, however, in their minds the connection is clear. They did not send a donation to Pat Robertson and then receive a cheque in the mail. They received a cheque in the mail *because* they sent a donation to Pat Robertson. It is a contingency miracle with a very plain and discernible cause, and there is no way the secular critic can dissuade the couple from the causal analysis they have decided on.

Financial healings and monetary miracles figure prominently on broadcasts of the '700 Club.' Clearly their main purpose is to legitimate the ministry and its actions and to encourage others to become participants in the faith. Though this class of miracles has something of the quality of a lottery about it, financial reward is promised only to those willing to make sacrifices in their lives. As in the preceding account, this frequently involves realigning one's financial priorities. By putting the '700 Club's' financial welfare ahead of one's own, one takes the initial step on the road that invariably leads to miracles. Jerry Falwell also demands this priority realignment with his mottos and gimmicks, including a lapel pin which reads "Jesus First." And Falwell is far less circumspect than other televangelists regarding the economics of this view of Christianity, arguing in his book *Listen, America!*, that capitalism is commended to us by God in the bible. Financial miracles, then, are the logical and divine result of sound capitalistic ventures.

The above miracle of financial salvation is important for other reasons. The cheque which this couple discovered in their mail after they posted a donation to the '700 Club' was not signed by God. In other words, how can one claim as miraculous the payment of money that was owed? Did they not know the cheque was on its way?

In *The Psychopathology of Everyday Life* (1901), Freud argued that many cases of apparent forgetfulness are actually motivated by unconscious wishes. For example, an individual may forget to keep an appointment with a colleague some days after the two exchanged angry words. The forgotten appointment is revenge taken by the unconscious, for by claiming the oversight to have been accidental, the forgetter is spared any serious pangs of guilt. Though the forgetful person in this case might see himself as too cool-headed and sophisticated to resort to such a childish display of displeasure, the wish for vengeance stirred by his anger was too powerful for the unconscious not to act upon.

For Christians who believe strongly in a God who performs miracles, the motivation to be the recipients of divine action can be powerful indeed. Hence if one "forgets" that a cheque is due in the mail, it is possible that the conditions which would make a miracle likely will emerge. Moreover, there is no need to impute conscious deceit to the recipients of the miracle, for the event may be entirely arranged by unconscious aims acting in concert with an overarching—and sometimes overwhelming—belief. To suggest deceit at all is perhaps to miss the

point. The structure of the fundamentalists' world—the socially
constructed reality in which they live (Berger and Luckmann, 1966)—
is governed by an internal logic which supports the system's central
precepts while suppressing the appearance of apparent contradictions.
Though it seems to the outsider that the miracle has been artificially
arranged, it is important to point out that all belief systems are constructed
out of certain underlying presuppositions. What the theist seeking a
miracle interprets as a causal sequence, the doubter perceives as
contingent. But if one shares the fundamentalists' beliefs, there is nothing
contrived about financial miracles at all. To get to such a point, however,
one must be prepared to make with Kierkegaard the leap of faith which
lands one in an entirely new belief system.

Thus miracles are appropriate events for supporting the
fundamentalist faith. Miracles also give the appearance of activity. They
show that God's power is presently at work, moving people, changing
lives, and strengthening the faithful. With miracles, the notion of the
"fundamentalist movement" is made less of an oxymoron, for miracles
add to the implied stasis of fundamentalism a dynamic dimension in
which change—albeit change is prescribed directions—is truly possible.

All of this is not to suggest that we can completely relativize the
fundamentalist condition and take their claims for miracles as merely
belief-specific interpretations. It is always necessary to retain a critical
position when approaching any claim for the supernatural.
Fundamentalism does not itself contain any critical discourse for dealing
with its internal affairs. Unlike science, humanism, and even other
religions, fundamentalism recognizes no gradation in belief or
commitment, no possibility of partial acceptance. The binary logic of
fundamentalism is total, and the mere suggestion that there is room
within its system for serious and critical inquiry will not be accepted.
Thus the task of adopting a critical stand falls to those who are outside
the fundamentalists' reality, as indeed it should with any system which
proclaims ontological and epistemological absolutism.

Financial miracles make evident the truth of Weber's thesis that
success in the financial world can both eliminate the theist's doubts and
verify that one is a member of the elect.[1] To claim a miracle in the
realm of finances by sending an account of that "salvation" to a program
like the '700 Club' is to demand public acknowledgement of your blessing;
it is to boast of material and spiritual success under the guise of pious
humility. And for CBN, telecasting a monetary miracle is proof of the
ministry's claims. Such testimonials are advertisements of the wisdom
in investing at the Bank of the Lord.

The Medium is the Miracle

The more well-known televangelists like Pat Robertson, Jim Bakker, Billy Graham, and Jimmy Swaggart have all proclaimed at different times that television represents potentially the single greatest evanglizing force in history. But in such proclamations, TV preachers have failed to realize that television acts not only as a medium of transmission, but as a medium of translation as well. This point has been made by many investigators, including Todd Gitlin:

Whether deceptively labeled as "entertainment," "news," "culture," "education," or "public affairs," TV programs aim to narrow and flatten consciousness—to tailor everyman's world view to the consumer mentality, to placate political discontent, to manage what cannot be placated, to render social pathologies personal, to level class-consciousness. (1972: 345)

In their zeal to appropriate television technology, evangelical preachers have been oblivious to the dialectical relationship inherent in any use of the medium, for to the extent that they have used television to spread the gospel, television has also had a significant influence on their theology. This has meant that religious programs have increasingly taken on the conventions and formats of mainstream, secular television. And thus the nature of what gets called a miracle on televangelist shows has been determined by the guidelines of what constitutes "good" television.[2]

As Jerry Mander (1978) has argued, television, like all media, is comprised of a series of inherent biases. For example, television newscasts normally present their "stories" in a confrontational mode, for television must find ways to express richly complex ideas in a black-and-white simplicity. Television has thus gradually developed the techniques required to package news, neutralize complexity, and make commodities of human lives. And no programming has remained immune, not even religious shows. In their quest for money and ratings, televangelists have turned their religion into an enormous self-parody, but a parody that plays well to a television audience. As Neil Postman has put it:

On television, religion, like everything else, is presented, quite simply and without apology, as an entertainment. Everything that makes religion an historic, profound and sacred human activity is stripped away; there is no ritual, no dogma, no tradition, no theology, and above all, no sense of spiritual transcendence. On these shows, the preacher is tops. God comes out as second banana. (1985: 116-117)

Postman's claim that television turns theology into entertainment cannot be denied by anyone who has spent even a few minutes watching Jim Bakker, Robert Schuller, or Pat Robertson. Televangelists have learned that to be "televisable," religion must sell, for television is, after all, a commercial technology. Thus TV evangelists, as Franklin Krohn has argued, have acquired the language of contemporary marketing:

As years have passed, television preachers have learned how to more effectively "package" their programs to be more appealing to their intended audiences. First, the preachers present their programs at times other than the traditional Sunday morning hours. Second, the visual impact of sparkling fountains, colorful floral displays, and magnificent architectural designs are liberally used. Third, "entertainment" in the form of celebrities, testimonials, and faith healing is offered the viewers. Fourth, the programs are designed to be interesting, exciting, and action-packed. Millions of dollars are spent to accomplish this more effective "packaging" of religious programs with a resultant larger audience and larger budgets than ever before. (1981: 52)

As Krohn suggests, televangelist miracles can be seen not only as events which legitimate and strengthen the religious ideas being broadcast, but they may also serve as tools of the marketer. Miracles may, in fact, be commercials. This view seems undeniable when one hears Jim Bakker declare, "We have a better product than soap or automobiles. We have eternal life" (Krohn: 55). Theology, in other words, is a product, and miracle testimonials are advertisements presented with the intention of demonstrating the value of the preacher's message. Moreover, these commercial-miracles are not always meant to sell the viewer on Christianity; frequently their aim is to induce brand loyalty in the individual preacher. Thus, for example, a woman who phoned the '700 Club' to pledge money said that since she had started watching Pat Robertson

her mentally retarded son was "getting better." Despite the fact that mental retardation is not a disease from which one "gets better," the genial Pat Robertson eagerly accepted the pledge with shouts of "Praise the Lord" and "Hallelujah." (Krohn: 59)

In 1924, Bruce Barton wrote that by miracles and other works, Christ "was advertised much more than by his words" (Barton, 1924: 137). Furthermore, Barton advised that "every advertising man ought to study the parables of Jesus" (146). Barton—himself an advertising man— intended no sacrilege by his comments, for he offered his claim that Jesus was the world's first advertising executive from the view of one fully committed to his Christian beliefs. One wonders, then, what Barton would have thought had he lived to see the uses to which marketing techniques have been applied in the sale of faith and miracles. To hear the televangelists tell it, every Christian's story of financial success is a miracle, including the creation of their own ministries. And even these organizations remain afloat only by the divine hand of the Lord. To show that this is actually so, some televangelists resort to highly ingenious schemes. For example, when Jim Bakker's 'PTL Club' built "Kevin's House," a home for handicapped children, it was announced that the construction needed to be completed in thirty days, a situation that would be impossible under ordinary, secular circumstances. Furthermore, Bakker announced, the house would also be debt-free on its completion date— another miraculous happening. Thus regular viewers of the 'PTL Club' were treated to what was called "Countdown to a Miracle." Here Bakker and his staff had actually set out the parameters within which God was to perform his miracle. More importantly, pressure was then placed on the ministry's supporters to make certain the miracle did take place. Each donation brought the miracle closer to hand, and each contributor could take pride in the fact that he or she was actively participating in the unfolding of a miraculous event. In the end, the construction did come in under the deadline, but unfortunately for Bakker there were outstanding bills to be settled after the structure was completed.

Peter Horsfield writes in *Religious Television: The American Experience*:

Images of success have always been important to the fundamentalist and evangelical traditions. Success in one's endeavours, indicated by followers, finances, or miraculous occurrences, is frequently understood and promoted as an indication that God is blessing one's enterprise. (1984: 101)

Horsfield's point is crucial. In American fundamentalism as that faith is practiced and promoted by electronic preachers, the concept of success has developed out of the action of two interlocking constituents: financial power and religious salvation. Hence the miracle recipient is granted dual citizenship in being saved: one passport to the Kingdom of God, and a second to the American Dream.

Miracle, n. An act or event out of the order of nature and unaccountable, as beating a normal hand of four kings and an ace with four aces and a king.—Ambrose Bierce.

Conclusion
In what may be an apocryphal story, it is said that when novelist Anatole France was shown the collection of discarded crutches and canes

in the shrine at Lourdes he turned to his guide and asked, "No wooden legs?"

The point is telling. No one who came to Lourdes seeking a miracle left with a newly grown limb. But for those with moderate ambitions who find Lourdes a far-away journey, a televangelist contingency miracle remains a real possibility. All that is required is allegiance to a literalist epistemology and a willingness to see divine presence in the most mundane of life's experiences. This will not produce a new leg, but it may see a lost pet safely home.

As I have argued, it is not an effective ploy to criticize televangelist miracles by expressing doubt over the actual occurrence of the miraculous event. Contingency miracles of the sort mentioned here do not yield to the empiricist's rigorous demands. The function of such miracles is not to astonish, for usually there is nothing astonishing to report. Because the citizens of the televangelists' world see themselves as under attack from the outside forces of the secular militia, televangelist miracles work to augment that religious community's sense of solidarity. The true function of televangelist miracles is to bolster the faith of the theists by strengthening their commitment to the socio-political agenda prescribed by their literalist reading of scripture.

As Berger and Luckmann (1966) have argued, each socially constructed world needs to discover or create some justification for its beliefs, and they call those phenomena which serve to legitimate a specific claim to truth "legitimating apparatuses." Miracles are legitimating apparatuses in that they show the theist what particular issues are presently of such importance that God would apply his divine hand to direct events to a specific end. Christian athletes are successful because competition is good; lost pets are returned to their owners because all life is sacred; and Christian businesses thrive because God is actually a capitalist. Though contingency miracles may appear mundane and lifeless at first look, they become vital forces for socio-political legitimation in the hands of TV preachers. Furthermore, this process of legitimation works in two directions, for in being saved not only does the theist acquire the belief system which makes possible the interpretation of ordinary events as miracles, he also finds that miracles are powerful forces for legitimating the belief system. What appears tautologous to the critic is sacred truth to the believer.

The slow but steady shift in emphasis from violation miracles to contingency miracles has had important consequences for the nature of televangelism. In the first place, it has substantially reduced the possibility of public scrutiny by dissipating the force of event-oriented critique. And without the weight of continual criticism pressing upon the faith, followers of the televangelist brand of religion are relieved of the burden of having to defend miracle claims which are eyed with suspicion in a world of increasing scientific knowledge and sophistication.

Second, contingency miracles achieve their status only in the context of the theists' faith. A shared interpretation is all but entirely immune from the challenges of those who stand outside the believer's world. In the gradual movement from violation to contingency miracle there has also been a concurrent retreat inward; whereas a violation miracle defies those laws that explain nature, a contingency miracle unites the faithful in mutual understanding. By claiming for themselves and their viewers miracles in the return of lost pets and the success of financial ventures, televangelists proclaim the social construction of a world in which ordinary events are accorded extraordinary significance.

In the process of emptying the miraculous of its magic and vitality, televangelists have found an effective means for engendering solidarity while further insulating their worldview from the larger sphere of secular life. What is lost in the realm of the sacred is gained back in the form of an electronic congregation which sends money, makes celebrities of preachers, and regards their own bank accounts and the World Series as potential sites for miraculous activity.

Still, it will be argued, televangelists cannot be said to use the word "miracle" to denote anything that would traditionally be regarded as miraculous. This is certainly true, but it is important to reiterate that because the TV preacher's contingency miracle is so utterly mundane, its value resides not in its capacity to astound, but in its efficacy as a latter-day myth. Televangelist miracles are often the very antithesis of the extraordinary. One is reminded of George Bernard Shaw's *Saint Joan*:

La Tremouille: Well, come! what is a miracle?

The Archbishop: A miracle, my friend, is an event which creates faith. That is the purpose and nature of miracles. They may seem very wonderful to the people who witness them, and very simple to those who perform them. That does not matter: if they confirm or create faith they are true miracles.

La Tremouille: Even when they are frauds, do you mean?

The Archbishop: Frauds deceive. An event which creates faith does not deceive: therefore it is not a fraud, but a miracle. (*Saint Joa.₁*: Scene II)

To have faith in the beliefs promoted by televangelism does not mean that God will perform miracles. Rather, what this faith promises is that the believer will be able to see miracles where none existed before. This may sound like deceit, but, as Shaw tells us, faith is capable of turning deceit into miracles. Perhaps this power of transformation is the real miracle of televangelism.

Thanks to Paul Antze, Rhonda Hammer, Cathy Hill, and Gerry Vise. Financial support for the period during which this paper was written was supplied by the Social Sciences and Humanities Research Council of Canada.

Notes

[1] "In conformity with the Old Testament and in analogy to the ethical valuation of good works, asceticism looked upon the pursuit of wealth as an end in itself as highly reprehensible; but the attainment of it as a fruit of labour in a calling was a sign of God's blessing" (Weber, 1904-5: 172).

[2] The '700 Club', for example, seems particularly partial to both financial and conversion miracles if they involve alcohol, drug abuse, violence, or criminal activity. Those viewers who are lucky enough to have their miracle presented on the '700 Club's' airwaves frequently reenact the divine episode for the cameras, thus committing to video tape the story of their conversion, financial blessing, or rescued pet. What is significant is that we are not told about the miracle but actually shown it—albeit as a docu-drama. Just as every news report needs a visual dimension (even if only in the form of stock footage), so too televangelist miracles are somehow made more real if turned into spectacles.

References

Barton, Bruce, (1924). *The Man Nobody Knows: A Discovery of the Real Jesus*. Indianapolis: Bobbs-Merrill.

Berger, Peter, and Luckmann, Thomas. (1966). *The Social Construction of Reality*. New York: Anchor Books.

Bierce, Ambrose. (1906). *The Devil's Dictionary*. Maryland: Stemmer House Publishers, 1978.

Falwell, Jerry. (1980). *Listen, America!*. New York: Bantam Books.

Freud, Sigmund. (1901). *The Psychopathology of Everyday Life*. Harmondsworth: Penguin Books, 1960.

Gitlin, Todd. (1972). "Sixteen Notes on Television and the Movement." *Literature in Revolution*. Eds. George Abbott White and Charles Newman. New York: Holt, Rinehart and Winston.

Holland, R.F. (1965). "The Miraculous." *American Philosophical Quarterly* 2: 43-51.

Horsfield, Peter G. (1984). *Religious Television: The American Experience*. New York: Longman.

Hume, David. (1748). *An Inquiry Concerning Human Understanding*. New York: Bobbs-Merrill, 1955.

Krohn, Franklin B. (1981). "The Language of Television Preachers: The Marketing of Religion." *Et cetera: A Review of General Semantics* 38: 51-63.

Mander, Jerry. (1978). *Four Arguments for the Elimination of Television.* New York: Quill.

Nietzsche, Friedrich. (1895). *The Anti-Christ.* Trans. R.J. Hollingsdale. Harmondsworth: Penguin Books, 1968.

Postman, Neil. (1985). *Amusing Ourselves to Death: Public Discourse in the Age of Show Business.* Harmondsworth: Penguin Books.

Rao, K. Ramakrishna. (1981). "Hume's Fallacy." *Journal of Parapsychology* 45: 147-152.

Shaw, George Bernard. (1924). *Saint Joan: A Chronicle Play in Six Scenes and an Epilogue.*

Weber, Max. (1904-5). *The Protestant Ethic and the Spirit of Capitalism.* New York: Charles Scribner's Sons, 1958.

Blessed Are the Rich: The New Gospel of Wealth in Contemporary Evangelism

Jill Dubisch and Raymond Michalowski

Introduction

Several years ago Tammy Bakker, the wife of T.V. evangelist Jim Bakker, relayed to their viewers the moving story of how she acquired a tape recorder. Early in her evangelistic career Tammy longed for a tape recorder to use to improve her singing voice so that she could better glorify God. She prayed fervently and repeatedly for that tape recorder, never loosing faith in her Good Shepherd. Then one day she opened her front door to find on her doorstop, not the morning paper, but— that's right—a tape recorder. Her prayers had been answered. God had interced in her moment of need and provided her with a token of his love in the form of state-of-the-art electronics.

Tammy's tale is just one of the many instances of the way in which modern evangelists, particularly T.V. and radio preachers, have come to incorporate contemporary materialist desires into their religious message and religious practice. Not only did Tammy get a tape recorder, but the Bakkers have been rewarded by the Lord in recent years with such things as a condominium in Florida complete with gold plated bathroom fixtures, a half-million dollar home in Palm Springs, California, a Rolls-Royce and a Mercedes Benz (The Charlotte Observer, Oct. 5, 1984). The Bakkers explain these luxuries as appropriate rewards for their evangelical work.

While the materialistic message of the Bakkers and certain other contemporary evangelists might be seen by some as antithetical to Christian values of piety and other-worldliness, this message is a meaningful one for the followers of this new brand of preacher. In order

33

to understand the apparent contradiction posed by such materialism within a religion that worships a god who chose to be born among the poor, we need to consider the meaning of this materialism for the followers of the new gospel of wealth both within the context of contemporary social experience and in relation to its historical roots in the long-standing uneasy relationship within Protestantism between materialism and spirituality.

Spirituality vs. Materialism: The Historical Roots

Almost from its beginnings Protestantism has alternately, and sometimes simultaneously, embraced and rejected worldliness and the search for material success. At the time of its emergence in late medieval Europe, Protestantism was closely linked to, and found its main supporters among, the rising bourgeoisie—a class whose interests lay in replacing feudal concepts of wealth and wealth-holding with a system based upon a competitive, rationalized meritocracy devoid of inherited privilege (Weber 1946). This is not to say that early Protestants were hedonistic materialists; early Protestant theologians in fact preached a severe asceticism focused on hard work, prayer and abstemious living. Although in the century following Calvin's rise, his theology of glorying God through hard work underwent a degree of secularization (Rifikin 1982), later Protestantism and Protestant preachers did not break totally with the more rigid codes of Calvin, and the emphasis on avoidance of hedonistic material pleasures remained a viable component of Protestant theology. But by the 17th century Protestantism had to contend with the growing concentration of private capital and the emerging ideology that wealth and property were both God's reward to the just and a sign of membership among God's elect. For example, the Laws Divine and Moral of the early Massachusetts Bay Colony initially specified that leadership could only be exercised by members of the religious elect, and at the same time established property ownership as the primary operative criteria for determining membership into the Puritan church of the elect.

This tolerance of material wealth sometimes revealed itself in a tension between preachers and congregations. Cotton Mather (1975:45), for instance, sermonized his opposition to a proposed law for debt relief in the Massachusetts Colony saying that "the grand cause of peoples running into debt is their unwillingness to bear the humiliations of a low and mean condition in the world," and instead seeking "lives lived in splendor." Mather's frustration with growing material desires was not the only or the last example of anti-materialist sentiment within

Protestantism. From the colonial period onward the emergence of religious and secular groups seeking in one way or another to re-energize the commitment to plain living has been a feature of American culture (Shi 1985). Many of these groups, such as the Quakers and the transcendentalists, were variants of Protestant thinking and found in scriptural writing the justification for their exhortations to a style of life that was less materially and more spiritually oriented.

With the rise of industrialization the tensions between materialism and spirituality both in Protestantism and in daily life intensified for several reasons. The transition to wage labor as the modal form of production necessitated a way of life based on the acquisition of commodities. The getting and spending of money rather than production for use become the central tasks of daily survival.

The growth of industrialization was dependent not only upon wage labor, but also upon creating a commodity-oriented populace. Early captains of the new mass production industries recognized that the expansion of production required replacing self-reliance with a desire for industrial commodities. It was in this period and in response to this need that the modern advertising industry was born. Despite the protestations of the advertising industry that it does not create demand but only responds to the need for product information, there is substantial evidence that this new information industry played an important role in promoting a commodity orientation within American culture during the latter part of the 19th century (Ewen 1978). Thus advertising raised the practice of consumption, already rendered a necessary part of life by the transition to wage labor, to the status of a desired and even worthy activity. That conscious and deliberate efforts were made to accomplish such a transformation is demonstrated by remarks such as those of a 1920's motivational researcher who said that it was necessary to demonstrate to the consumer that the "the hedonistic approach to life is a moral, not an immoral one" (Shi 1984:249).

A key component of advertising was the repeated message that social acceptability was contingent upon appropriate commodity consumption. As the new world of commodities and advertising began to link material display to social acceptability, social acceptability and religiosity began to be separated. That is, it became increasingly possible to see oneself— and to be seen by others—as a socially acceptable and worthy person simply by living a certain *style* of life. Religious performance and practice began to play an increasingly secondary role in the emerging definition of social acceptability in the post-industrial commodity-oriented world. Emerging social images equated success with material success and morality with material consumption. Thus judgments about personal worth that previously had primarily been framed in terms of morality and religiosity were now made in the context of the secular world.

Linked to this is the appropriation by advertising of many elements of religious imagery and symbolism. The image of transcendence became secularized as the marketers of materialism began to promote their wares as representing the "ultimate," as "heavenly," "divine" or in the words of one ad as "the final step up." What had previously been reserved for religious text now became part of secular, material discourse.

From the religious side there were two responses to the new world of commodity promotion and consumption. One was a reassertion of the simple life. The other was an incorporation of materialism within the framework of religion, both symbolically and as a design for action. The message that materialism and godliness are not only not necessarily antithetical, but can in fact exist in a sympathetic relationship with one another had become a distinct sub-category within Protestant preaching by the end the 1930's. One of the best examples of the unification of materialism and spirituality in the American tradition is Russell Conwell's popular sermon "Acres of Diamonds." Conwell is quite explicit about the link between materialism and morality. He says, for instance:

I say you ought to get rich and it is your duty to get rich. How many of my pious brethren say to me, "Do you a Christian minister spend your time going up and down the country advising young people to get rich, to get money?" Yes, of course I do.... Because to make money honestly is to preach the gospel. The men who get rich may be the most honest men you find in the community.

In recent times this theme has grown in scope and prominence and has become a characteristic component of the message promulgated by many contemporary media preachers.

The Theology of the Gospel of Wealth

The contemporary gospel of wealth is not simply an opportunistic injection of materialist ideology into Protestant theology. Rather it represents an ordered theological text which claims its authority from scripture. The text of the contemporary gospel of wealth exhibits three main characteristics: (1) It establishes God's concern with the material world of his followers and his efficacy as a source of personal wealth and/or success. (2) It provides a set of prescribed actions for personal material success. (3) It offers a theological explanation for the poverty and misery in the world today which insulates the successful from guilt in the face of those problems.

God and personal wealth. The first element of the gospel of wealth is to dispense with the idea that God is either opposed to or not concerned with the material life of Christians, and to substitute in its place the idea that personal success in the material world is part of God's plan. Rev. Kenneth Hagin, for instance, begins his pamphlet *Obedience in Finances* with the scripture "My God shall supply all your needs according to his riches in the glory by Christ Jesus." (Phil. 4:19) Rev. Don Stewart (1980:xvii) in his book *Miracle Happiness* says in the introduction that, "God has a Master Plan for your life. That plan provides a powerful and practical way for you to have all your needs supplied...." Several pages later, like Rev. Hagin, he offers Phil. 4:19 as proof that God's Master Plan includes providing materially for his followers. This idea of success as God's sign of special favor to his elect is similarly represented by former Miss America Cheryl Pruett, "I think God's people *should* be Miss Americas and presidents, *should* be the people who run things.... They *should* be successful and have money. It's only right" (Helgesen 1985:262). In the same vein as Pruett, Rev. Stewart (1980:17) directly addresses what he sees as the mistaken notion that poverty is in any way looked upon favorably by the lord. On this point he says, "There is absolutely no virtue or value in material poverty."

Rev. Pat Robertson (1982:35), the founder of the 700 Club and the Christian Broadcast Network, finds his basic text on God's material beneficence in the New rather than the Old Testament. He offers Matthew 6:33 which ends "and all these things shall be added to you," to theologically ground his argument in *The Secret Kingdom* that God is the route to material success. Or in his words (1982:60):

Now when God blesses us and keeps us, and lets His face shine upon us, and is gracious to us, then before men we appear in a light that far transcends any of our natural abilities. He can cause our plans to succeed. He can cause people to like us. He can cause us to be preferred and chosen above others of equal talent. He can protect our children. He can guard our property. He can cause His angels to aid us.

This is clearly a God who intervenes in the material life of his followers, even to the point of subverting equal opportunity employment. Robertson goes on at this point to give testimonial to the role God played in securing for him 3 million dollars worth of electronic equipment for his CBN ministry.

Robertson (1982:58) elaborates his theology of wealth by saying that the very first thing we must know about "how God's kingdom works" is that "there is absolute abundance in the Kingdom of God." No matter how bleak economic situations may look for individuals, nations, or even the world, there are no actual barriers to their resolution, according to Robertson, since God is in control of a storehouse of unlimited abundance that can alleviate *any* situation of material need. As one example Robertson (1982:74) notes that while it is clear that we will exhaust our supplies of fossil fuels some time in the future, we need not worry since we have "big oceans" and in all likelihood God will "give to one or more of his people a concept for running cars on such water." To skeptics who doubt that this is physically possible Robertson's (1982:61) answer is that God "is above the laws of nature and any restrictions that those laws might try to impose."

The essence of these texts is that God clearly does speak about the material world. By identifying references in scripture to the material world—or, what they interpret as references to the material world—the preachers of the gospel of wealth seek to establish, first of all, that religiosity is not only a matter of the spirit, but a plan which pertains to a successful life in the secular world as well. Kenneth Hagin's *How to be a Success in Life* is perfectly clear on the worldliness of God's rewards:

I'm interested in the here and *now*. I need help for my hurts *now*. I need something *now*—not future "pie in the sky",... I want to know what can happen to me *now*.

Jesus Christ said that if we'd get into the Word, we could have success in our lives now. (emphasis in original).

It is through texts of this sort, and through testimonials of the material benefits procured through God's agency that gospel of wealth preachers seek to create an image of a god that responds to the everyday material concerns of the faithful, as well as to their spiritual needs.

The Gospel of Wealth as a Plan for Action. The gospel of wealth is not simply a get-rich-quick scheme. It presents instead a long-term plan for action by which the faithful can benefit "in due season" (Hagin 1982:21) from God's abundance. As presented by gospel of wealth preachers this plan attempts to rectify the tension between materialism and spirituality in Protestant theology.

According to the gospel of wealth, while God can provide, he will do so only and most abundantly for those who make God's will and not material success their first priority in life. "Godliness insures prosperity" in Hagin's words. However, one must undertake the twin tasks of accepting the will of the Lord and toiling diligently to fulfill that will in order to "have total favor with the ruler of that abundance," in the words of Robertson's second principle of how God's kingdom works. The full text of Matthew 6:33 upon which Robertson builds his case is, "But seek *first* His kingdom and His righteousness; and all these things shall be added to you" (emphasis added). The key to God's storehouse of abundance then, is "determining God's will and then doing it on earth" (Robertson 1982:61). The route to having God become your "Source and Supplier" is to "put God first in your life," says Stewart (1980:11). The godly life that will bring reward, material as well as spiritual, "calls for a total yielding of the reins of life from one's own hands to God's hands" (Robertson 1982:81). And Hagin uses the following story to show that submission to God's will pays off, in the here and now:

> At a seminar I was holding...God told me to give away the airplane that Kenneth Copeland had given our ministry. (It's worth about $160,000 to $170,000). I gave it to Brother Jerry Savelle.
> Several weeks ago, a man I don't even know...wrote in and said, "We feel led of the Spirit to send you this check for $500,000." That's half a million dollars, glory to God!
> I'm well satisfied that if I hadn't obeyed God, that wouldn't have happened, yet I didn't have that in mind when I obeyed God and gave away the...airplane. I really didn't expect anything in return.

Frequently the gospel of wealth presents in the same text, as in the case above, testimonials and promises of God's reward to those who do his will, along with the teaching that we should submit to God's will without expectation of reward. This coupling of the discourse of selflessness before God's will with examples and promises of the favors showered upon those who have done God's will exemplifies the theological tension inherent in attempts to link material and spiritual realities into a unified perceptual schema.

The second component of the plan for action in the gospel of wealth is the principle of toil. The adage that "God helps those who help themselves" occupies a prominent position in the social philosophy of the gospel of wealth. In *How to be a Success in Life* Kenneth Hagin Jr., son of the Rev. Hagin quoted previously, relates an exchange with his father that illuminates this principle. The younger Hagin complained that while he and his family had clothes, furniture and a car, that was all, and he wanted to "build up something for my family." His father responded by saying:

> It's the problem a lot of people have. They're always talking about prosperity, but they've never put their hand to anything.... Son, you've got to get out and start *doing* something. You've got to do something for the Lord to prosper you." (emphasis in original)

The younger Hagin with a firm resolution to do something, "got involved in a real estate investment," began to "pray about it," and in a year's time had a financial statement that "showed an enormous return on that small investment." Lest you mistake this success as purely a matter of good financial wisdom, Hagin, Jr. points out that this kind of success can only be expected by praying and entering into business with other Christians.

The idea of work in the gospel of wealth is usually linked to the notion of *giving*. In a turnabout similar to those who follow God's will with no thought of reward, those who work hardest out of a desire to give to others, rather than from a desire to be successful, will be the most successful. Both Robertson (1982:103) and Stewart (1980:137) utilize Luke 6:38—"Give and it will be given unto you..."—as the basis for their theology of work. The giver ends up the receiver.

This notion of the selfless giver who receives has been translated into the current secular philosophy of capitalism. George Gilder, one of the architects of the new Republican right, bases his apologia for capitalism on the proposition that the capitalist, the investor, is a giver. Every act of investment is a gift to society made without certain expectation of reward (Gilder 1981). Thus any contradictions between Christianity and capitalism are erased and the supposed naked pursuit of money becomes, in effect, a religious act.

If giving is not rewarded swiftly, this is no cause to doubt God's promise according to the new gospel of wealth since another component of the concept of toil within the gospel of wealth is perseverance. All of the documents we examined offer testimonials of how long hard toil in the fields of the Lord and retaining faith when things looked darkest were *eventually* rewarded. In Robertson's (1982:139) words:

Some Christians have been taught that all one has to do to get things from God is to speak the word of faith, believe, and receive. That comes close to the truth, but it neglects the universal Law of Perseverance. God slowly yields the good things of the kingdom and the world to those who struggle.

Functions of the Gospel of Wealth
Why has this theme of material success come to be such a prominent feature in at least some of the current evangelism? It is easy to reach the cynical conclusion that it is simply a way for evangelical preachers to justify their own conspicuous consumption while simultaneously attracting followers. But even if we dismiss the preachers themselves as not really believing what they preach (often an unfair charge), we still need to explain the continuing loyalty of the followers who presumably

do believe. In order to do this, we need to examine first several important features of religious belief systems.

Anthropologists studying religion have often emphasized religion's role in the construction of systems of meaning. Such systems involve both belief and a plan for action and they attempt to bring together the *is* and the *ought*, the way the world is perceived to be and the way it should be (Geertz 1966). In a changing world, such meaning systems are in constant need of revision, revitalization, reinterpretation, and occasionally overthrow, as people attempt to come to terms with new conditions which do not fit old ideas (Wallace 1956).

In surveying the history of the relationship between Protestantism and materialism, we see a movement away from the idea that wealth results directly from work which is itself a reflection of godliness (i.e., work is a virtue practiced by the religious) toward the belief that wealth comes through godliness alone (which may require work as a sign of faith and commitment but the work itself is not the source of wealth). Socially, this is paralleled by the movement from wealth based on the activities of merchants, landowners, and entrepreneurs to the contemporary route to success through management. Management is not an occupation directly related to any form of material production; the product, in a sense, is really oneself and requires packaging in a manner suitable for marketing in the business world. Success manuals for managers emphasize the importance of self-presentation ("dress for success") and of one's ability to manipulate interpersonal relationships. (These are really two sides of the same coin.) In a similar vein, the religious route to success, as preached by certain contemporary evangelists, requires that one "get right with God." Cheryl Pruett, Miss America 1980, exemplifies both the secular and religious aspects of success. Beauty contests could be considered the ultimate marketing of the self and the Miss America contest is, of course, the pinnacle of beauty contests. Cheryl Pruett had faith in God and in her own ultimate success and "considered winning the title to be her personal destiny" (Helgesen 1985: 260).

We would like to draw a parallel here, in some ways perhaps far-fetched but in other ways illuminating, between the new gospel of wealth and another religious phenomenon observed by anthropologists, a type of religious movement known as cargo cults.

Cargo cults are religious revitalization movements which occur in certain areas of Melanesia and Miconesia. They are a response to situations of colonialism in which local peoples see their traditional culture disintegrating and in which they experience simultaneously the political and military dominance of whites and the influx of desirable European and American consumer goods. Cargo cults develop when a leader arises who preaches that his followers should return to the old ways (or some variation thereof) and refuse to cooperate with whites. Members of the cult then build airstrips or piers which will accommodate the planes and boats laden with consumer goods ("cargo") which will be sent by the ancestors once the whites have gone. Fantastic as these cults seem, they make sense within the perceived reality of a people who are experiencing the pressures of colonial domination and who have no conception of the industrial society which produces white goods and which underlies white political and military power. "Cargo" in this context becomes both a symbol and a cause of power. A cargo cult, then, is a logical attempt to both explain and remedy an intolerable situation. (For a general discussion of cargo cults see Worsley 1968; what we have presented here is a simplified description of a complex phenomenon.)

We can see the new gospel of wealth in a similar light, as appealing to people who feel the pressure of what they view as a moral disintegration of American life yet who do not wish to forsake the possibilities for material affluence which that way of life offers. The answer is to return to the ways of the ancestors, to godliness as outlined in the scriptures. This will then lead to the downfall of the ungodly and to the material abundance which is God's intended state for his elect. Financial well-being, as one author tells us, is received through faith and through supernatural manifestations of the holy spirit (Hagin 1983). It is "cargo," sent not by the ancestors but by God.

Anthropologist Clifford Geertz has pointed out that one of the perennial problems with which religion must grapple is the gap between what is and what ought to be. Some live in poverty while others flourish. The image of success is held up to all yet many fail to attain it. One answer to this dilemma is the gospel of wealth, which explains failure as well as success: "...if a person is *continuously* in sickness, poverty, or other physical and mental straits, then he is missing the truths of the kingdom" (Robertson 1982: 75). For Miss America, the key to success is simple: "what we *think* controls what happens in life so I always make sure to think *yes*" (Helgesen 1985: 262). If God has not blessed your finances, it is because you have not enough faith, you have not sowed the seed (Hagin *Obedience* 2). In fact, to be sympathetic to those who are unsuccessful may be interpreted as contrary to God's plan. "God don't support no flops" reads the sign over the kitchen table in Miss Pruett's family home (Helgesen 1985: 261). And if others are poor, it is because they are unworthy and hence they deserve their poverty. This is further articulated in the following quote from Pat Robertson:

> Despite our preconceived attitudes toward social justice, God's Law of Use controls the ultimate distribution of wealth. We must be willing to take the world as He made it and live in it to the fullest. For He says, in fact, that if we are willing to do that...we will have more. But if we are not willing to use what He has given us, we will lose it (1982: 124).

An earlier work, *Acres of Diamonds* is even more pointed: "...the number of poor who are to be sympathized with is very small. To sympathize with a man whom God has punished for his sins...is to do wrong...." (Conwell 1982: 21)

These statements illustrate one of the oft-noted characteristics of belief systems, including that of the gospel of wealth, and that is their self-validating nature. Beliefs do not simply develop directly or inductively out of experience, but instead exist prior to such experience and shape our interpretation of it. The examples of God's supernatural manifestations of material abundance sprinkled so plentifully in evangelical preaching serve to confirm the belief system; if such manifestations fail to appear to you, it is because you do not have the necessary faith, not because the beliefs themselves are faulty.

At the same time, evangelists themselves often serve as validation of what they preach. Though constantly attacked by the media for his extravagant lifestyle and pursued by the FCC for alleged misrepresentations in his fund-raising telecasts, Jim Bakker's appeals for money never failed to draw a response from his faithful viewers. Heritage USA, though ridiculed by some as a "Christian Disneyland," has nonetheless become one of the most-visited theme parks in America. Why do Bakker's followers not resent his condo in Florida, the Rolls Royce, the gold bathroom fixtures? Why do they not find hotels, water slides, and stores selling Tammy make-up incongruous with a Christian message? The answer, we suggest, lies in what these things represent in the context of the continuing tension between spirituality and material success which has characterized Protestantism throughout its history. To their followers, the Bakker's personal affluence is both a just reward for godliness and a promise of what they too can acquire. And Heritage USA is an image of the material benefits which God's faithful can enjoy on earth. And television is, of course, the perfect medium for this message since it is the great shaper and conveyer of material images of American life. At Heritage USA the heavenly kingdom is no longer something to be realized only spiritually and in the hereafter; it exists to be enjoyed here and now. Thus Jim Bakker's "Christian Disneyland" serves to reconcile the conflict between the spiritual and the material, between this world and the next. And through their offerings, his followers can invest in that vision. In fact, they can, if they wish, purchase through a single payment a lifetime of vacations at Heritage USA.

As Jim Bakker's continuing monetary troubles indicate, his construction of God's kingdom on earth rests on an unsteady financial base. But this is not inappropriate. We could argue that in both cargo cults and in the new gospel of wealth there is a lack of recognition or acknowledgement of the inevitable requirements and concomitants of the industrial way of life that ultimately produces material wealth. Yet at the same time there is a desire to enjoy the material benefits of that way of life. While such an attitude may seem either self-serving or naive, we must take into account that for both the Pacific islanders and for many people in our own society there is a lack of experienced connection between the goods they enjoy and the work which produces them. The shift to service jobs, the assembly line nature of production— these mean that most people do not see the making of a product in its entirety from start to finish; indeed they seldom see the making of any part of that product at all. New cars, VCR's, tape recorders, computers—all appear as magically in the stores for our consumption as Christmas presents appear under the tree for a child. Is it any wonder then that for the godly they might just as well mysteriously drop from the sky, and that, in effect, some preachers promise that they will.

Movements such as cargo cults and evangelism based on the new gospel of wealth are more than just ways in which their followers try to understand confusing or threatening social forces and more than just a means of personal aggrandizement. The gospel of wealth utilizes the American ideology of free enterprise while at the same time seeking to preserve a role for spirituality in an increasingly secular and materialistic world. It does this by interposing God as the mediating agent between work and reward. In this way the gospel of wealth provides a statement of hope of, as well as a blueprint for, a new order, one that in the eyes of its proponents promises to be more just and rewarding than the one in which they currently live.

References

Conwell, Russell
    1982 reprint of lecture; (Burlington, Ontario: Inspirational Promotions Inc.)

Ewen, Stewart
　1978 *Captains of Consciousness: The Social Roots of Advertising* (New York: McGraw Hill).
Geertz, Clifford
　1966 Religion as a Cultural System. *Anthropological Approaches to the Study of Religion*, ed. Michael Banton, New York: Frederick Praeger.
Gilder, George
　1981 *Wealth and Poverty* New York: Basic Books
Hagin, Kenneth
　1982 *Obedience in Finances* (Tulsa: Kenneth Hagin Ministries Inc.)
　1983 *Godliness is Profitable* (Tulsa, Kenneth Hagin Ministries Inc.)
Hagin, Kenneth Jr.
　1984 *How to Be a Success in Life* (Tulsa: Kenneth Hagin Ministries)
Helgesen, Sally
　1985 Here She Is, Miss America. In *Popular Writing in America* (3rd ed.), eds. Donald McQuade and Robert Atwan (New York, Oxford University Press) (originally published in *TWA Ambassador*, July, 1980).
Mather, Cotton quoted in
　1975 William E. Nelson, *The Americanization of Common Law* (Cambridge, MA: Harvard University Press, 1975).
Rifikin, Jeremy
　1979 *The Emerging Order: God in the Age of Scarcity* New York: Putnam
Robertson, Pat
　1982 *The Secret Kingdom: A Promise of Hope and Freedom in a World of Turmoil* (Nashville: Thomas Nelson Publishers)
Shi, David
　1985 *The Simple Life: Plain Living and High Thinking in American Culture* (New York: Oxford University Press, 1985)
Stewart, Donald
　1980 *Miracle Happiness.*
Wallace, Anthony F.C.
　1956 Revitalization Movements. *American Anthropologist* LVIII: 264-281.
Weber, Max
　1958 *Protestant Ethic and the Spirit of Capitalism.* New York: Charles Scribner's Sons
Worsley, Peter
　1958 *The Trumpet Shall Sound: A Study of Cargo Cults in Melanesia.* New York: Shocken Books.

Exorcism of Fools
Images of the Televangelist in Editorial Cartoons

Edward H. Sewell, Jr.

The editorial cartoon, as a communication medium, presents brief visual messages couched in images that can be quickly processed by the viewer. The tools of the editorial cartoonist must lend themselves to simple but powerful visualizations and include stereotype, metaphor, exaggeration, and myth.

The editorial cartoon as a form of mass communication can be traced back to the advent of the printing press in fifteenth and sixteenth century Germany. One of the first major uses of the cartoon for editorializing was in the religious upheavals we collectively call the Protestant Reformation. The images used were based on common experiences or invented relationships. Thus, Martin Luther was presented as an intemperate fellow with beer mug in hand and bloated belly in a wheelbarrow filled with fellow heretics and followed by his ex-nun wife holding their illegitimate child, *sola fide*.[1] Another image, from the titlepage of a work done by P. Sylvius in 1535, depicts Luther in the process of forming a pact with Lucifer. With one hand on the Bible, and the other hand holding Lucifer's hand, an agreement is being sealed.

The editorial cartoonist in the sixteenth century, and his counterpart in the twentieth century, work within what Victor Turner calls a "liminal" environment.[2] They work on the margins of acceptable journalism in that while their work does not fit the traditional roles of reporter or editor, their visual images appear on the editorial or comic pages of the newspaper. Their role is that of a clown or trickster not unlike that of the court jester in medieval society. They play the fool, but a fool who makes fun or play with the serious matters of the court. In this liminal position, the editorial cartoonist has greater freedom to comment on important topics in ways that would bring cries of libel

46

Luthers vnd Lutsbers
eintrechtige vereinigung / so in rrij
eygenschaffeen sinde allenthalben gleychförmig verfüget/
Durch M. Pet. Sylvium der Chenlenbert in seliger warnung trewlich
beschriben vnd mit Göttlicher schrifft vnwidersprechlich ergrün/
det. wie es am lersten blat ist volkomlicht berdet.

Anti-Lutheran Propaganda Cartoons.

if they were used in a news report or even a written editorial. It is the freedom of liminality that gives rise to new images and metaphors or creative insights where the cartoonist or other liminal person has "a certain freedom to juggle with the factors of existence."[3] Liminality provides the cartoonist with a power or potency which represents a "limitless freedom, a symbolic freedom of action...where the elements of culture and society are released from their customary configurations and recombined in bizarre and terrifying images."[4]

The fool or court jester embodies several functions that we see embodied in the work of the editorial cartoonist.[5] First, the fool serves as a corrective to those people who claim more than their due, who are pretentious. Second, the fool represents over-conformers as people who become ludicrous because of their enthusiasm. Finally, the fool serves as an acceptable outlet for aggressive tensions that build up in society. The editorial cartoonist is intentionally critical and intentionally makes light of serious claims and pretentious people. Steve Kelley, editorial cartoonist for the *San Diego Union*, defined editorial cartoonists as "the guys who sit high above the political battlegrounds and watch the fighting. Then when that's all done and the smoke begins to clear, we come down from the hills and shoot the wounded.... The cartoon is journalistically antithetical to everything the editorial page represents. In a carefully-posted hospital zone of expression, the cartoonist has been given keys to a bright red Ferrari. Should he confine himself to the designated limit, or gun the engine, squeal the tires, and see just what he can do?"[6]

The new technology of the twentieth century is television, and like the new technology of the printing press in the sixteenth century, it has created an irony described by Goethals as "the emergence of a technological sacramentality" that has "returned its proponents, unconsciously perhaps, to a dependence upon a physical as well as spiritual mediation of grace, bringing them full circle to the dependence upon image and object that the sixteenth-century reformers so vehemently rejected."[7] The visual epitome of this "technological sacramentality" is contained in a cartoon by Doug Marlette formerly of the *Charlotte Observer*.[8] With halo and pious grin Jim Bakker, host of the PTL Club (PTL stands for "Praise the Lord"), appears on the screen of a television set. He says, "Blessed are the T.V. evangelists—for they shall inherit the Gold Coast condo!"

Let us now turn our attention to an analysis of how editorial cartoonists have treated several major religious leaders. The editorial cartoonist works as the court jester of the modern-day newspaper. For the televangelist, he serves as a print media critic of their televangelistic programming. The religious leaders to be considered are Billy Graham, Pope John-Paul II, Jerry Falwell, and Pat Robertson.

Billy Graham in Moscow

Billy Graham, "Preacher to Presidents" and the premier of the televangelists, took a trip into the heartland of Communism in 1982. The editorial cartoonists followed his trip, and drew commentaries focusing on the plight of imprisoned Christians in Soviet Russia, the mother of atheism.

The scriptural injunction to "comfort the prisoner" provided a primary image for the editorial cartoonists. In a dark and medieval-like Soviet prison, cartoonist Steve Benson of the *Arizona Republic* introduces us to two Russian Christians who are in chains. From a radio we hear this simple message: "This is Brother Billy Graham on Radio Free Moscow, reminding all Soviets in Christ to obey the authorities...." The cartoon seems to imply that Billy Graham does not realize the plight of some "Soviets in Christ," or perhaps even that he chooses to overlook their dire circumstances for the sake of a successful evangelistic effort.

Cartoonist Bob Gorrell of the *Richmond News-Leader*, formerly of the *Charlotte News*, drew a similar cartoon in which he shows us a solitary "Soviet religious prisoner" who is representative of the oppressed religious groups. This prisoner, chained by the neck and hands is staring blankly into a bowl. His rations for the day seem to bring him little comfort as he questions his meager helping of "Graham crackers?"

For those Soviet Christians fortunate enough not to be in prison, Billy Graham delivered several sermons in historic Moscow churches, both Russian Orthodox and Baptist. In keeping with true southern hospitality, he extended the invitation, "If y'all are evah neah Montreat, N.C., y'all drop by, heah?" Etta Hulme, cartoonist for the *Fort Worth Star Telegram*, shows us a Billy Graham who seems to be oblivious to the realities of life in the Soviet Union.[9] Can he really stand there with Bible in hand and overlook the fate that awaits this dejected and beaten-down Soviet Christian? It is almost as though Billy Graham does not realize that this is not television hype. Will the rerun look any better?

Just as Luther consulted with Lucifer, so Billy Graham consulted with an earthly Lucifer while in the Soviet kingdom. Cartoonist Dwayne Powell of the *Raleigh News and Observer*[10] pictures Billy Graham at the bedside of ailing Soviet leader Leonid Breshnev. We break into a conversation in progress and see Breshnev hooked up to life-support equipment and Graham sitting at his bedside with hands folded in a

" BLESSED ARE THE T.V. EVANGELISTS— FOR THEY SHALL INHERIT THE GOLD COAST CONDO!"

Figure 2 . Cartoon by Doug Marlette of the *Charlotte Observer*. Reprinted by Permission.

Figure 3

Cartoon by Bob Gorrell of the *Richmond News-Leader*

Reprinted by Permission

Figure 4

Cartoon by Etta Hulme of the *Fort Worth Star Telegram*

Reprinted by Permission

holy prayerful position. We can but guess what has been said in the conversation, but it might have sounded like one of Graham's televised sermons. Breshnev has listened to the Gospel message, and now we hear his Soviet-bound response: "So much for that other hogwash...tell me more about the second coming!" Billy Graham does not respond with the Christ-like injunction to this earthly devil to "Get thee behind me Satan!" No, Graham's only response seems to be a smug grin.

From presidents to premiers, the familiar image of the friendly televangelist and magnetic preacher of worldwide crusades bears little resemblance to reality. Has he been duped by several decades as a successful American religious broadcaster? The editorial cartoons about Graham picture him as one who provides us with an acceptable outlet for aggressive tensions generated between our free society and the closed Soviet society. While we cannot act on our aggressive impulses toward the monolithic anti-religion society of the Soviets, we can use the internationally recognized televangelist as the scapegoat who takes a trip into the depths of an earthly "hell" to consult with the Russian "devils." We can release our emotional ammunition and then forgive Graham because we know that he truly is doing the "Lord's work."

John-Paul II as Super-Pope

The leader of the Roman Catholic Church, Pope John-Paul II, has moved out of the cloister of Vatican City into the world of media hype taking on himself the image of "super pope" who travels the globe. He has shown us that under the gown of Holy Mother Church lives a fun-loving and powerful man. Editorial cartoonist Pat Oliphant reminds us that people who share the common life of religious leadership are quite human. John-Paul II is planning his next trip to the United Kingdom, but his mind is also thinking of even more distant trips.[11] In a conversation with one of his Vatican advisors, John-Paul II wonders, "I don't know if I should also go to Buenos Aires...perhaps we should send Billy Graham." The real point of this cartoon comes not from the papal conversation for in the lower right-hand corner of the cartoon is a verbal aside placed into the mouth of Puck, Oliphant's alter-ego. Puck says, "Yeah-Billy doesn't see much!" The reference is, of course, to Billy Graham's recent trip to the Soviet Union, a trip we examined in the previous section of this paper.

But one must be careful not to underestimate the power of the Pope, for before him even Communist leaders shrink in fear and submission. Tony Auth of the *Philadelphia Inquirer* shows the Pope using a simple cross to defeat the evil spirits of international Communism. Yet this

Figure 5

Cartoon by Steve Benson of the *Arizona Republic*
Reprinted by Permission

Figure 6

Cartoon by Mike Keefe of the *Denver Post*
Reprinted by Permission

same Pope who can exorcise the evil spirits seems at times to have just
a hint of some evil spirit within himself. Steve Benson of the *Arizona
Republic* depicts an encounter between John-Paul II and a bishop of
the Church in Central America. With a friendly greeting, the marxist-
leaning bishop says, "Heyyy, Pope Baby. The Church welcomes you
to Central America!... Death to the imperialists!! (he kisses the Pope's
outstretched hand) Long live the Marxist Revolu—" The bishop said
the wrong word, and in a spirit of papal rebuke, John-Paul plants his
fist firmly on the bishop's chin. As he passes on by, the Pope comments,
"The devil made me do it."

Pope John-Paul II is a very televisual personality, and he often
chooses appropriate opportunities to catch the eye of the television camera
as he delivers an important message. At times, it seems, he even creates
a pseudo-event just for television consumption. Cartoonist Tom Toles
of the *Buffalo News* focuses on the Pope delivering a simple message.[12]
John-Paul II says, "The needs of the poor must take priority over the
desires of the rich.... Workers must participate in decision-making and
receive a greater share of profits...." The next frame of the cartoon
reveals that what appeared to be a live speech is really a televised speech,
and as we watch the televised papal message, we see and hear with a
somewhat different perspective. "The poor shall judge the rich who amass
to themselves the imperialistic monopoly of economic and political
supremacy." The final frame of the cartoon lets us in on the real secret
of the cartoon—we are not the only ones watching this televised papal
message. No indeed, there watching this speech with us is none other
than President Ronald Reagan. Reagan's response to the speech is simple
and revealing, "Better not let *him* write our school prayer."

While Pope John-Paul II is not your "typical" televangelist, he works
well within the infrastructure of an electronic "global village."

Jerry Falwell and the Moral Pejorative

Our third televangelist is quite unlike either Billy Graham or John-
Paul II. His pulpit is based in Lynchburg, Virginia, and his television
ministry focuses on the standard Baptist worship service with a good
dose of politics thrown in for good measure.

What better image than the famous painting, "American Gothic,"
to introduce us to Rev. Jerry Falwell, founder of Moral Majority and
super-television evangelist. Cartoonist Pat Oliphant used this image to
make a statement about the fuzzy line between the religious and the
political in Moral Majority.[13] The farm home in the painting has become
a church with a sign out front reading "The Jerry Falwell Church of

Figure 7

Cartoon by Dwayne Powell of the *Raleigh News and Observer*

Reprinted by Permission

Figure 8

Cartoon by Clyde Wells of the *Augusta Chronicle*

Reprinted by Permission

the Moral Pejorative—A Tax-Free Organization." Standing in front of the church is Justice Sandra Day O'Conner with a pleasant smile on her face. Next to her with pitchfork in hand stands a sour-faced self-righteous Jerry Falwell with his Bible in hand. The caption, obviously a statement from Rev. Falwell, reads, "Supreme Court, indeed! Get back in your place, woman!" The power of the video-image coupled with the power of the God-image seems to have corrupted absolutely, for now this mild-mannered pastor from semi-rural Virginia can make pronouncements about nothing less than the composition of the Supreme Court of the United States.

Mike Keefe, editorial cartoonist for the *Denver Post* draws Uncle Sam in dire straits, for standing atop a "King Falwell Version of the Bible" is the Moral Majority, jumping up and down in an attempt to shove the book down Uncle Sam's throat.[14]

As Jerry Falwell says his bedtime prayers, cartoonist Pat Oliphant draws the image of self-righteousness extended to its logical extreme.[15] On the bedside table is a Micky Mouse lamp and a Bible. Over the bed hangs a photograph of Falwell clutching his Bible with holy gumption. And Falwell prays: "We thank Thee for the gifts of Thy bountiful herpes and Thine blessed AIDS, O Lord...now send us something for all the other weirdos." Not only is God into conservative politics, but now He seems to be on the frontline of medical intervention services.

In the end of the matter, we come once again to that familiar image of televangelist Falwell cooperating with the devil or one of his assistants. Cartoonist Dwayne Powell lets us eavesdrop on a conversation between Falwell and a visitor to his office. On Falwell's desk is a nameplate that reads,

Moral Majority, Inc.
Rev. Jerry Falwell, Honcho

Sitting beside his desk is none other than old Lucifer himself, and a rather medieval-looking Lucifer at that. Falwell is reading a list supplied by his evil guest, "...and you were against the canal treaty, you support an arms race, were against recognizing China...by golly, you're not as bad as we thought!" This Rev. Falwell with fake halo and plush chair appears quite Luther-like in his unholy alliances.

Pat Robertson: Prayer, Power and the Presidency

The televangelist-of-the-hour is, of course, none other than Pat Robertson of the Christian Broadcasting Network. From his television studios in Virginia Beach, Rev. Robertson fights off the evil destruction of hurricanes, hosts a television call-in prayer program, and engages in familiar conversations with God about whether to run for the office of President of the United States. What a target for cartoonists!

Already several of the "Doonesbury" comic strips by cartoonist Garry Trudeau have been pulled from newspapers in Virginia and Iowa.[16] The first offensive series of comic strips featured Pat Robertson holding a press conference, but this was not your ordinary press conference because Robertson was curing reporters of various ailments including hangnails, hernias, and hiccups. Then to top it off, Robertson goes on record, "The Lord God has personally asked me to consider running for president!" Star reporter, Rick Redfern, comments, "Beats an endorsement from the Teamsters." In a later strip Trudeau has Redfern at home watching the Christian Broadcasting Network evening news. Emanating from the television set we hear the voice of Ben Kinchloe, co-host of the "700 Club," saying, "That's it for news on Christian Broadcasting Network. Here now with the weather is Pat Robertson." The voice of Pat Robertson picks up with, "Thank you, Ben! . . . Tonight we command a low pressure front to bring 2" to 4" of rainfall to the drought-stricken southeast." There is an on-air "Amen!" Pat continues, "We also ask the Lord God for a cooler air mass to trigger steady showers in the northern plains states, and may the snow flurries in Idaho not stick, but melt." Another on-air response, "Melt, Lord!" The weather report, as prophetic command, continues until Robertson finally says, "I'll be right back to arrange the 5-day outlook after this." We once again hear the voice of Ben Kinchloe, "Friends! Need rain in your area? Support Pat's Accu-prayers by . . ."

While Trudeau has been the most vicious of the cartoonists in his treatment of Pat Robertson, others have not been shy in their attacks. Mike Keefe of the *Denver Post* characterizes Robertson as removing his halo in order to cast it into Uncle Sam's presidential-hopeful hat in anticipation of the 1988 elections.

Steve Benson of the *Arizona Republic* pictures the Robertson for President headquarters. We notice that on the walls are slogans such as "Pray, Pay, Obey." There is also a poster of Jesus and Pat (halo included) in a very campaign-like pose with the title "Vote the Team." We are allowed to eavesdrop on a telephone conversation between a Robertson for President worker and an unidentified caller. The Robertson worker says, "We are reaching out with Christian love for all denominations—especially fifties and hundreds."

On the same theme, campaign contributions, Clyde Wells of the *Augusta* (GA) *Chronicle* draws a cartoon of Pat delivering a speech. Pat says, "Send me a sign so that we may embark upon this glorious quest." As a dollar bill in the form of a paper airplane flies past, Pat remarks simply, "Thank you."

Collegiate editorial cartoonist, A. J. Stone of the Virginia Tech *Collegiate Times* lets us overhear a telephone conversation between Robertson and an unidentified caller. The microphone-laden lecturn is adorned with a simple sign reading

PAT
God's Choice

A caption at the top of the cartoon says, "...televangelist Pat Robertson announced his intention to run for president, saying that God told him to." Robertson standing behind the lecturn, telephone to his ear, and a smile on his face says, "...one more thing, boss...they want to know if they can quote you..."

Figure 9

Cartoon by A. J. Stone of the *Collegiate Times*
Reprinted by Permission

Blessed Are the T.V. Evangelists

We have seen in these few examples how several editorial cartoonists are carrying on the age-old tradition of the court jester making fun with serious topics. Perhaps we feel better ourselves for having let them say things that we would like to say, or perhaps we have become irate or at least a little angry over something they have said. Whatever the case, they have worked to correct the pretentious tendencies in the televangelists. They have made the over-zealous ludicrous. They have allowed us, the readers, to vent our emotional tensions in ways that are socially acceptable. They have surveyed the battlefield of religious broadcasting, taken on the most visible knights of televangelism, and engaged them in a joust-for-the-fun-of-it combat. They have spoken in images where words would be potentially libelous, and they have had a good laugh while doing it.

Notes

[1]This particular image from the late sixteenth century was based on an earlier broadsheet by Hans Weiditz. For a more complete discussion of the broadsheets and images of the Reformation, see R.W. Scribner, *For the Sake of Simple Folk: Popular Propaganda of the German Reformation* (Cambridge: Cambridge University Press, 1981); G. Strauss, *Luther's House of Learning: Indocrination of the Young in the German Reformation* (Baltimore: Johns Hopkins University Press, 1978); and N.L. Roelker, "The Impact of the Reformation Era on Communication and Propaganda." In H.D. Lasswell, D. Lerner, and H. Speier (eds.), *Propaganda and Communication in World History*, vol. II, (Honolulu: University of Hawaii Press, 1980).

[2]Victor Turner, *The Ritual Process: Structure and Anti-structure* (Chicago: Aldine Press, 1969), p. 125.

[3]Victor Turner, *The Forest of Symbols: Aspects of Ndembu Ritual* (Ithaca: Cornell University Press, 1967). p. 106.

[4]Victor Turner, "Myth and Symbol." In *International Encyclopedia of the Social Sciences*, vol. 10, p. 577.

[5]For a complete treatment of the history of the fool see O.E. Klapp, *Heroes, Villains, and Fools* (Englewood Cliffs: Prentice-Hall, 1962); and W. Willeford, *The Fool and His Scepter: A Study in Clowns and Their Audiences* (Evanston: Northwestern University Press, 1969).

[6]Steve Kelley, "The Ungentlemanly Art of Political Cartooning," a speech given at the Illinois Press Association, September 26, 1985.

[7]Gregor Goethals, "Religious Communication and Popular Piety," *Journal of Communication, 1985, 35:153.*

[8]Doug Marlette, *It's a Dirty Job... but Somebody Has to Do It!* (Charlotte, NC: Willnotdee Press, 1984), p. 142.

[9]The cartoon is found in Charles Brooks (ed.), *Best Editorial Cartoons of the Year 1983* (Gretna, LA: Pelican Publishing Company, 1983), p. 123.

[10]Dwayne Powell, *Surely Someone Can Still Sing Bass!* (Raleigh, NC: The News and Observer Publishing Company, 1981), n.p., cartoon dated October 9, 1980.

[11]See Pat Oliphant, *Ban This Book!* (Kansas City: Andrews and McMeel, Inc., 1982),

p. 158.

[12]Tom Toles, *The Taxpayer's New Clothes* (Kansas City: Andrews and McMeel, Inc., 1985), p. 86.

[13]Pat Oliphant, *The Jellybean Society* (Kansas City: Andrews and McMeel, Inc., 1981), p. 178.

[14]The cartoon is found in Charles Brooks (ed.), *Best Editorial Cartoons of the Year 1982* (Gretna, LA: Pelican Publishing Company, 1982), p. 144.

[15]Pat Oliphant, *The Year of Living Dangerously* (Kansas City: Andrews and McMeel, Inc. 1984), p. 20.

[16]See *Editor and Publisher*, September 20, 1986. The two newspapers were the *Richmond Times-Dispatch* and the *Cedar Rapids Gazette*.

The Blessings Of Billy

Marshall W. Fishwick

"I am only a Western Union boy carrying God's message."

Billy Graham

In March, 1938 a nineteen-year old student at the Florida Bible Institute finished his evening walk on the eighteenth green near the school's front door. (Bible Institutes seldom have golf courses—this one was a reconverted country club, purchased cheaply during the Depression, and it had one). "The trees were loaded with Spanish moss," he remembered later, "and in the moonlight it was like a fairyland." Suddenly he fell to his knees, and said, "O God, if you want me to preach, I'll do it."

He did it. William Franklin Graham has been heard by more people (live and through mass media) than any preacher who ever lived. For over thirty years he has been *the* world-wide voice for evangelical Christianity; the epitome of popular mass religion.

It is easy to parody Graham, hard to fathom him. Taken out of context, single events or statements of his life are easy game for the Smart Set. But the total context of his life—and his continuing influence not just for years but for decades—is impressive. Presidents, popes, and pop singers come and go—Billy Graham remains. He sings and talks of the "Rock of Ages—" and is himself, for millions, the rock of this age. Of whom else can that be said?

"As I look back over my life," Billy Graham writes in *Angels: God's Secret Agents* (1975), "I remember the moment I came to Jesus Christ as Savior and Lord. The angels rejoiced! As I yielded my will and committed myself totally to Christ—as I prayed and believed—I am convinced that God 'put a hedge about me,' a hedge of angels to protect me."[1] From all indications, those angels have done an excellent job.

His origins are humble enough. Born in 1918 on a North Carolina farm, raised in a conservative branch of the Presbyterian church, Billy attended church regularly. When he didn't pay close attention to the

Billy Graham—Grand Old Man of Televangelism.

sermon, his father whipped him with a leather belt. Young Billy listened, memorized the entire Shorter Catechism, and joined the church when he was twelve. His "decision for Christ" came four years later, in a temporary tabernacle where the fiery Mordecai Fowler Ham preached fire-and-brimstone in the piney woods and made the Devil cringe. But Ham's most famous convert was not ready to sell Christ—he chose instead to peddle Fuller brushes, door to door. Two life-long friends, Grady and T.W. Wilson, remember details of this first calling.[2] "Billy was the most dedicated salesman the Company ever had," they testified years later. Billy (by then Doctor) Graham explained: "I had become convinced that Fuller brushes were the best in the world and no family should be without them. Selling those brushes became a cause to me...a matter of principle."[3] Billy's quick success as a salesman got him the right to be called upon to instruct other salesmen in the techniques of selling. To his mother he once remarked: "Women...need brushes and now I'm going to see that they get the chance to buy them."[4] A few years later the Wilson brothers would once again team up with Graham to sell what they were convinced is not only the best religious faith in the world but the *only* genuine faith. Millions have agreed, forming a network that literally reaches around the world.

Billy Graham's life is a parable of American righteousness. He represents, better than any other human being, Mid-America since World War II: high pastor of the proud and mighty of a mighty proud land. There is a library by and about him: most of it, in the words of an astute observer and biographer, is largely parochial, repetitive, and thin.[5] Graham emerges as a long, lanky cliche: an animated manikin. What makes Billy run?

The oft-repeated tale of that run (or, more accurately, climb, up the ladder) can be quickly summarized. Pastor of a Baptist church in his mid-twenties, Graham was asked to take over a Sunday evening radio program on Chicago's WCFL. This went well, and he was asked to preach at the "Youth for Christ" rally. Another success—on the road he went, wearing loud hand-painted ties and carrying Southern style preaching deep into Yankee territory and Canada. He even toured Europe and converted thousands. His first major city campaign in America (Los Angeles, in 1949) proved to be pivotal. Few could have predicted it. The Committee was reluctant to give him a larger tent and a $25,000 budget; but at the end of three weeks the revival suddenly caught on. Many credit William Randolph Hearst's order to his editors to "puff Graham." Others point to Stuart Hamblen, a cowboy singer and radio talk show host. When he announced his conversion on the radio show, crowds flocked into the Canvas Cathedral. So did Hearst's reporters and photographers. The Los Angeles *Examiner* and the *Herald Express* used banner headlines. Their dispatches, carried by Hearst papers across the country, were picked up by the Associated Press. Jim Vaus, a prominent underworld figure and wiretapping expert for gangster Mickey Cohen, was converted. Olympic track celebrity and World War II hero who had since become poverty-stricken, Louis Zamperini, followed shortly afterward. *Time* and *Newsweek* both featured the "new evangelist." Headlines across the country played up the conversions. The crusade finally closed on November 20, 1949. The tent, enlarged to seat 9,000, overflowed with the largest revival audience since Billy Sunday's New York campaign of 1917.

The thirty-year-old sensation's preaching style was simple. Avoiding emotionalism, Graham followed the musical warm-ups with intense but flowing sermons heavily punctuated with quotations from the Bible and focused on contemporary public crises and personal problems. The atomic bomb became a favorite rhetorical device representing insecurities, and the spread of Communism was pictured as an increasing crisis and threat in world affairs. Graham was and is in tune with the times. This intense trumpet-lunged prophet found the right chord, and has never stopped playing it. We are living in a time when God is giving us a desperate choice: revival or damnation.

On and on he rolled. In 1952, at the close of his five-week Washington Crusade, a special act of Congress enabled Graham to address a rally on the steps of the Capitol building and to have that address carried live by radio and television. He became a personal friend of Lyndon B. Johnson and Richard M. Nixon. In 1952 Graham also met with President Harry Truman, attended both national political conventions, spent Christmas with American troops in Korea, and was called by President-Elect Eisenhower to meet with him privately in New York shortly before his inauguration.

By then it was obvious that while Billy Graham might have only one God, he had two faiths: Christian Fundamentalism and Christian Americanism. Not that he was "selling his soul" to his national religion— a notion that would and does shock him. Instead, he maintains the shell of Christian Americanism in order to put life and spirit into it. By supporting civil religion he hopes not only to combat both humanism and agnosticism, but also to use it as a springboard for leading people into the evangelical faith.

Graham fears the challenge of humanism. He thinks that if its influence can be held in check, he will have a better chance of converting people to what is the one and only way for all mankind. This is why he strongly supports Bible reading and prayer in the public schools. They will combat humanism and increase the probability that young people will be more inclined toward accepting the evangelical faith which Graham characterizes as "personal faith in Jesus Christ."

The success of Billy Graham's strategy is seen in the way General Dwight Eisenhower moved increasingly from a vague religion of "Americanism" to a definite evangelical faith. In December 1952 the General said: "Our government makes no sense unless it is founded in a deeply felt religious faith—and I don't care what it is." A month later he joined the National Presbyterian Church. His views became more clearly evangelical as he spoke of Christ as the Son of God and of the Deity of the Bible as the true Creator. When Graham visited him shortly before his death, the General asked how he could know that his sins were forgiven and that he would go to heaven. Graham reminded him of the biblical answer and Eisenhower responded that he was ready to die.

One reason for the enormous and continuous success of Graham's crusades is the simple, direct points he hammers out so that no one (not even presidents) can miss them. His own foreign policy (in an age of extreme complexity) is simplistic. One proposition says it all: without God, America and the free world will probably be destroyed. But if all Americans would repent and turn to Christ, whom Graham presents as America's final hope, then "we would have divine intervention on our side." There is little doubt that in the 1950s, Graham's version of Christianity included the doctrine that America was the land which God had prepared for a chosen people. Rugged individualism was considered the mark of both patriotism and spirituality.

Largely uncritical of the McCarthy "Red Scare," Graham wanted to destroy "the rats and termites that are subversively weakening the defenses of the nation from within." He saw himself as the Joshua of Christian America. Like Joshua, he was afraid that when America's reputation slipped, so would God's. How could this be remedied? By doing what the Israelites did to Achan and his family: crush them with stone, then burn them with fire. Root out evildoers.

The popular use of the word "sickness" to describe the condition of an entire nation is an appealing way to bring medicine and theology into a single focus. The danger is that it implies the need for drastic surgery—with some blood for an angry God. This blood-letting may be symbolic and mythic. Abraham Lincoln died on Good Friday and, in the minds of many, symbolically atoned for the nation's great sin-sickness. Martin Luther King and the Kennedys are more recent atonements. Billy Graham is reported to have said in 1968, "If being shot or killed would glorify God, I'll be glad to go." Graham added that he almost hoped that he would have an opportunity to suffer for the sake of the Gospel.

At such moments, and in such statements, popular religion reflects its ability to adjust to new moods and understandings. The nation that confidently sent men to the moon couldn't free hostages held by a group of radicals in Iran. Men who had solved global problems seemed unable to cope with smog control and rain and school busing. Hence Billy Graham's "American Christianity" in the 1980s is quite different from what it was in the 50s or 60s. He has become increasingly sensitive to his cultural and social milieu at home and abroad. He no longer identifies Christianity exclusively with the West, or Communism with the East. What does not seem likely to change is Graham's conviction that he finds in the Bible word from the Almighty. Were that to go, what would be left? If *we can't trust the Bible*, what *can* we trust?

In insisting the Bible is infallible truth from God, Billy Graham has added some special interpretations. For example, he holds that before coming to earth Jesus had no body, whereas now He does. Today that body sits at the right hand of God the Father. In Graham's own words, "There is a Man at the right hand of God the Father. He is living in a body that still has nail prints in His hands." On Johnny Carson's *Tonight* show Billy Graham explained that a Christian entering heaven would be able to distinguish God the Father from God the Son by the nail prints in the hand of the Son. Whether this entails that the Father also has hands, feet, knees, beard, and other bodily parts is not clear.

What *is* clear is that Graham and Company are media-masters. Using the Johnny Carson show is just one note on their extensive keyboard. Radio launched Billy as a media-star; it might still be his best *personna*. He is heard every day on radio. Those who miss his voice can ponder his words in a daily syndicated newspaper column, *My Answer*; or they can get his magazine, *Decision*, which circulates in the millions. (Exact figures are hard to come by—my own inquiry brought the reply "well over six million.") Then there are the television crusades, films, satellites, videotapes, and everything electronically new and viable. Yet all these figures and media outlets don't answer the crucial question: how *does* the "miracle" of mass conversion take place? Watch Graham himself at work, and you get at least a partial answer: a time-tested formula, meticulous (almost military-like) planning, high theater, and endless follow-up. Just as it takes hundreds of unseen participants to stage a grand opera, political rally, or bowl game, so with a Billy Graham Crusade.

Since television has become his most extensive and effective ministry, and his telecasts can reach into nearly every American home, let's examine how Graham uses that hour, and how he actually comes across. When Graham was interviewed by the New York *Times* in 1957, he told precisely what he wanted:

"I would have someone like Fred Waring's orchestra and glee club playing and singing old religious hymns. Then a five to eight minute skit emphasizing a moral or spiritual truth. And then an interview with a famous person such as Roy Rogers or vice-President Nixon who would tell of his spiritual experience. This would be followed by a sermon. The program would be produced on the same scale as a major entertainment show."

Graham's television success has been closely tied to his live crusades in both style and distribution. Graham's 1954 Greater London crusade from Harringay pioneered the use of post office land-line relays to transmit Graham's voice to rented auditoriums scattered throughout England and Scotland. For the 1957 Madison Square Garden crusade, the Bennett agency worked up a contract with ABC to broadcast eighteen Saturday night sessions on national television. The live quality was a great improvement over the 1951 telecasts, and more than 1.5 million letters, including 30,000 decisions for Christ, came to Graham. God—and the tube—had blessed him.

No one in the "organization"—least of all George Wilson, Billy Grahams' top "action man" since the Youth for Christ work in the 1940s—takes credit for all this. Billy's success is the will and the work of the Lord. Billy is clay in God's hand, the agent taking only a small commission to keep the crusade functioning. The real help comes from on high.

Much of the work has been done, and events planned to the split second, when the crowd gathers. The seeds have been well sown. This is harvest time.

The formula has been tested, tried, and fine-tuned. Year after year, country after country, the crusade goes on—Western Europe, Australia, India, Southeast Asia, Africa, and Latin America have all been fed into a complex computerized feedback system that records conversions, distributes follow-up literature, sends local churches converts' names and addresses, solicits and records contributions, and co-ordinates the multiple function of the Billy Graham Evangelical Association. Nothing except the "Decision" itself is left to chance. . .or should we say, to God?

A generation after the 1957 New York *Times* interview, the crusade telecasts (generally there are three a year) have changed little, though the pace is more relaxed. We open with long shots of the gigantic crowd while the sound track carries gospel hymn music (on youth nights, folk music). Then the camera pans on singers in the choir, and the audience. Titles are superimposed identifying the building, city, and state. In strides the master of ceremonies, Cliff Barrows, who exudes good cheer, welcomes everyone, and makes the opening sales pitch for Bible-study books. (Barrows, who joined the Graham team in 1949 when he was 22, also directs the choirs, which generally feature more than 1,000 voices.) Then an "outsider" comes forth to endorse and localize the crusade. An early favorite for this spot was Roy Rogers, often accompanied by his horse, Trigger; but now Roy has a different calling and sells fast food. During this "warm up period" four or five songs are also performed, often led by George Beverly Shea, who has been with the organization since 1944. If they are available, "celebrities" like Jerome Hines, Anita Bryant, or Ethel Waters might do a hymn. All this is *free*—although Barrows reminds you that only "your" contribution makes it possible.

Then, the moment everyone has waited for. In strides Graham, his Bible held tightly against his chest, chin resolutely lifted, with that immaculate glamor of Sunday-morning certitude, that look of a blond prince out of a Nordic fairy tale. He stands before the master console (custom-made for him by IBM) as waves of thunderous applause sweep over him. When it finally subsides, he speaks: "All the applause and all the wonderful things that are said will be stored up in Heaven and given to whom it belongs—Jesus!" Then the applause is repeated.

At just the right moment, the message. "It's almost as if I'm not even aware of the thousands and thousands of people out there," Graham says, "I'm preaching just to the first six inches in front of my face. I feel almost totally alone. And if nobody responded, if no one came, I would still preach."

So he *does* preach—for exactly 36 minutes, after which he asks listeners to make a total decision for Christ, then come forward to the foot of the speaker's platform. (It's the old "Action Seat" technique, used by Charles Grandison Finney more than a century earlier.) Then Graham folds his arms, reverently bows his head, and waits.

Not so with the team. Hundreds of well-trained counselors keen-eyed and full of "proof texts" from the Bible, quietly move down the aisles, ready to answer any question, then accompany the convert on that difficult march forward, one-on-one. Nor is the spoken decision enough. Each convert is taken into a counseling room where he fills out a card of personal information. This is sent to his or her local church— with a copy to BGEA headquarters. Within the next 48 hours, the counselor will follow up with a visit, call, or letter. The decision made that moment will not soon be forgotten—not so long as the computers respond.

The hour is almost up. One of the most important events has yet to take place: the call to the television watchers. Turning to the camera (watch cue cards!) Billy stretches out his arms (as Bernini did for St. Peter's in Rome, symbolically, when he designed the colonnade) to all the world. "You too can make the decision, if you will." He requests that you write to "Billy Graham, Minneapolis, Minnesota," and offers to send television converts the same material going to those who walked forward on camera. As he gives his final benediction—"God bless you—" up music, and pan the podium and crowd. Then the master of ceremonies, Cliff Barrows, comes in with a voice-over, repeating the call to the television audience. A picture of an envelope to Graham fills the screen. Another blessing, and credits superimposed over the last shots of the arena. The hour is finished—on the last second.

BGEA has delivered once again. They know their audience, and they have reached it: mainstream popular industrial culture, geared to contemporary needs and issues. Everything said, sung, and done has been within the framework of the dominant cultural assumptions of most listeners—and the power structure of those who make political and economic decisions. Graham provides the most powerful endorsement imaginable of the status quo by defining ultimate religious and moral issues as individual, private concerns. With him, Christ and culture go together like love and marriage, or coffee and cream, Peter and Paul.

The formula has world-wide appeal. Few places have responded as well to the Graham Crusade as Australia; nor was his work there cut off from mainstream America. The Global Village likes Global Evangelism. Billy's 1969 Australian Crusade, carried by 292 American television stations, brought in a bumper crop of converts at home as well as abroad.

The use of motion pictures, though less dramatic, has had a major impact which seems on the rise. BGEA has produced more than three dozen feature films. New ones are in the works. As a result of the media blitz, Graham receives more than 2 million pieces of mail annually, keeping the more than 400 employees in his Minneapolis headquarters hopping. They operate the BGEA on an annual budget of many millions.

Billy Graham capitalizes on each mass medium in his role of preacher to the masses.

The scale and scope of all this, which increased rather than decreased during the Reagan years, is more *mass* than *popular* culture, although Graham does attempt to avoid overt signs of mass manipulation and to provide a degree of personal inspiration and supervision over his association. Nevertheless, the elements of mass culture are omnipresent in Graham's approach—a standardized product; average taste; a large, heterogeneous, anonymous audience; developed not *by* the people but *for* them by an organized computerized marketing operation.

In the early years Billy's spot as "top evangelist" and mass media counterpart was contested by another Protestant (Norman Vincent Peale) and a Roman Catholic (Fulton J. Sheen). Sheen wrote more books— he published 80—but is dead now, and Catholicism has taken new roads since Vatican II. Peale lives and limps on—but the power of his "positive thinking" languished in the nation that went through Vietnam, Watergate, and the Age of Aquarius. Who was Graham's chief media-rival after 1965?

We need a good comparative study of Hugh Hefner and Billy Graham as media manipulators. Hedonism and evangelism do not have the same goals, but they certainly use many of the same devices and appeals. They are both very much a part of our age. Might they not both be reactions to, and off-shoots from, deep-rooted American Puritanism?

By 1985, in any event, the Bunny Hoppers were faltering but the God Pumpers were flourishing. Graham's Worldwide Pictures are just that—and contributions are tax-deductible. Their studios stand bigger and better than ever along a stretch of Burbank's Buena Vista Boulevard, just a stone's throw from the Walt Disney film factory. Worldwide owns its own Hollywood-style office building and sound-stage packed with the latest movie-making equipment. The people who work there are among the best in the industry and are paid accordingly. Making films for Billy Graham is considered a highly professional assignment.

How many people actually *see* them? Here one must trust Graham's publicists. The relatively unknown film called *The Restless Ones* has, say its sponsors, been seen by more than 4 million people—of whom 300,000 were inspired to make "the Decision" once they left the theater. More recently, Graham's films have had glittery Hollywood-style premieres, complete with celebrities, engraved programs, searchlights, and special police details. At the 1975 opening of World-wide's *The Hiding Place*, the prestigious Beverly Theater was filled with anxious, beaming first-nighters eager to see and be seen. In the ranks were "stars" and "personalities" with easily recognized faces, reputations, and connections. When the tumult and the shouting die, the multi-million dollar keeps on working, day after day, media after media—the richest and most powerful gospel organization the world has ever seen.

Over the Organization towers Graham. Did anyone ever *look* more like Hollywood typecasting? Tall, thin, with piercing blue eyes and flowing hair, using dramatic gestures and sounding like the blast of a bugle, he is superb. Even Charlton Heston, who got the Ten Commandments (on film) from God himself could hardly upstage Billy, who seems heaven-sent for the Billy Graham Crusade.

But he is not set in steel or chiseled in marble. He can and does adjust his "God consciousness"—not only his message, but his clothing (which has become much more conservative and business-like than in his early days), contracts, issues, and predictions. Only his success is monolithic; everything else is negotiable.

In the summer of 1984, the Graham team visited six English cities, drawing well over a million people (almost 3% of England's adult population). I was in England at the time and experienced the excitement. The conversion rate, averaging more than 9% of total attendance, was double the 4% at similar meetings across the United States. An average 55% of those going forward in Britain registered a "first-time commitment," rather than a "rededication" or to "seek assurance," higher than the usual 35 to 40% at Graham meetings. Over 60% of British inquirers were under 25 years of age, a higher proportion of youth response at Graham meetings elsewhere. Calling the mission "one of the most historic and momentous in our entire ministry," Graham said: "Never have people in such large numbers gathered in England to hear the gospel."

Even this achievement paled beside his evangelical tour of the Soviet Union. Earlier he had preached throughout Eastern Europe; in 1982 Graham attended a Moscow peace conference, and set off one of the major controversies of his career. Saying he found freedom for preaching and worship in packed churches delighted Russians and angered Westerners. Graham got permission to come back in 1984—a triumphant return.

Piotr Konovalchik, the pastor of Leningrad's only Baptist church, wiped tears from his eyes as he welcomed this American. "We know what difficulties you faced in coming here, Billy Graham," said Konovalchik. "We rejoice that you are with us tonight." Many young women in the choir, clad in orange dresses and white headbands, wept too. As Graham thanked Konovalchik, a clergyman from Moscow went to the pulpit to offer a prayer: "You shed your blood for Russia too, O Lord. We pray that a surge of revival may start in this house of ours."

It was the emotional high point of the American evangelist's most improbable mission since he went on the road for God: his first evangelistic tour of the Soviet Union, a country zealously committed to the extirpation of religion. Commented Graham en route to Leningrad: "I look on it as remarkable that I am here at all, preaching." Lenin would no doubt have agreed.

Churches were full wherever he went—some with visitors who had come 2,000 miles from Central Asia. In Tallinn, Estonia's capital, an overflow crowd of 3,000 stood in the streets outside the Baptist church. Translated phrase by phrase by interpreters, Graham's sermons were generally familiar, but the words had special power in the context of militant state atheism: "Jesus Christ is not dead on the Cross. He is a living Christ. He can come to your person. He can come to your family. He can come to your great country." This time there was no propaganda harvest for Radio Moscow. Instead, Graham assured the Soviets that Americans and President Reagan desire peace. But he consistently and deftly attached his hopes for world peace to the need for divine intervention—in his oft-used phrase, "peace with God."

Returning to the United States, reporting on his trip, Billy pointed out that all fifty church meetings in the U.S.S.R. were filled to overflowing—even those in central Siberia. "They never told me what to say. This is only the beginning of a new dialogue—perhaps even a new peace offensive." Only the party was committed to atheism—not the government, and certainly not the people. Graham believed they were ready for a religious revival—which their officials understood.

Could *this* be the same man who, early in his career, had condemned the "Godless Communists," and been closely identified with the Red Scare? What had happened to "the old Billy Graham?" No one, looking in from the outside, can say. He has listened, learned, and changed with the times. The young zealot has become the mature statesman. His style has mellowed.

Might he be getting soft—could he have been used by the Russians as part of their propaganda program? Graham replied that the Russians weren't using him, but he was using the Russians: to preach the Gospel and hear the word of God. "My trip opened up tremendous doors," he stated. With President Reagan having his first talk with a high-level Russian that same week, one could only speculate on whose medium was whose message.

Billy Graham's victory in the churches of Russia, and Reagan's in the polling booths of America, showed that the cult of personality, so long scorned by the Counter Culture and the chronicles of the "New Age," was alive in the mid-80s. The "Crisis of Confidence" which Jimmy Carter had described in 1979, "striking at the very heart and soul and spirit of our national will," was over. Perhaps these matters are cyclical. There were "Eras of Good Feeling" after the War of 1812, the Civil War, World War I, and World War II. Once again (with Viet Nam and Watergate fading and losing their bitter taste) America was up-beat. "The very fact that we would like things to be better is what's important," wrote theologian Harvey Cox. Flag-makers agreed. The Art Flag Company of Manhattan a major national distributor, reported a sales increase of 30% for 1984.

At the Hartford Crusade in 1985, Graham was much more calm, low-key, questioning than the fire-eater I remembered from my own student days. He was less prone to give answers, more ready to ask questions. The fire was still there but it was more controlled, even rationed. Cliff Barrows, Program Director since the first major Crusade, was still there; so was Tedd Smith, pianist since 1950. Most of all, there was the beloved bellow of George Beverly Shea, who has "sung the Gospel around the globe" for more than 30 years, and who was elected to the Gospel Music Hall of Fame in 1978. Seeing them in one evening had a *deja vu* effect. The country and the world have changed so much. The Graham people have changed little, and the old-time hymns they belt out ("Trust and Obey," "His Name is Higher," "He Is My Reason for Living") not at all.

The same meticulous arrangements which have always marked the Graham Crusade are still in place. Special provisions are made for the deaf, handicapped, elderly. Messages boards, Lost and Found, Crusade Books tables, ground crews, ushers, concessions are fully manned. Buses park free, as do cars at the Aetna Insurance and Travelers Insurance Company parking lots. By merely filling out a convenient form, one can get *Decision* ("A monthly inspirational magazine filled with helpful articles") for a whole year free. Prayertime broadcasts and the Follow-up Ministry have been organized for months. God is in the details.

We need to understand Billy Graham because we need to understand ourselves.[6] His changes are our changes; his hopes our hopes. Consider that central pillar of popular American religion, rugged individualism. Graham uses it less and less now; he prefers the term silent majority. Former rugged individualists now form a large block within America and see themselves as the backbone of true and genuine Americanism.

In them, Christian Americanism is thought to be the heir of this great
new land of Zion. They are the spirit of '76, the American Way embodied
in flesh and blood and Fords. But recently this sort of Americanism
has grown defensive. The old missionary zeal has cooled. Toyotas have
come to town. The Lord God of hosts did not give swift and sure victory
over the powers of evil in Vietnam. Sometimes it becomes difficult to
draw the line between the forces of God and of evil. Furthermore, the
American nation as a whole seems hesitant to succumb to another seizure
of McCarthyism. Although the silent majority itself is more myth than
reality, it does symbolize a new tone and base for popular theology.
One high priest, Richard Nixon, has been deposed; Graham is still very
near the altar.

   Astute at reading the public's mood, Graham has now found a new
war and a new enemy, a multiheaded monster—crime in the streets, dope
in the schools, sex everywhere. In this sense he has become (consciously
or unconsciously) allied with the new Republican president—Ronald
Reagan. Christian Americanism (unlike Roy Rogers or Gene Autry) is
back in the saddle again.

   For all their zip and zest, they are not young men. In 1987 Graham
is 69, Reagan is 75. At ages when most people have retired, they command
two of the most important roles and responsibilities in the Western world.
They are both poor boys who made good—true believers for whom the
American Dream Machine ground out power and plenty. But do they
still speak for our culture and our nation? Are they defenders of yesterday?
Are they in touch with the young? More important, are they in touch
with the world? We must wait and see and hope. To study Billy Graham
is to trace the mainstream of popular theology for half a century.

Notes

[1]Billy Graham, *Angels: God's Secret Agents* (New York: Doubleday, 1975), p. 174.
Graham has published a dozen books, and thousand of pieces in newspapers and magazines,
over the years. *Calling Youth to Christ* (1947) summarized his early work, *Revival in
Our Times* (1951) pointed the direction he would take, *Korean Diary* (1953) put forth
his international outlook, and *The Jesus Generation* (1971) was his answer to the Hippie
Generation. His syndicated column, "My Answer," began in 1952, and within a year was
reaching 15 million readers. How much of all this is ghost-written? Others prepare drafts;
but Graham claims he always reworks them "until they are mine."

[2]Quoted in Alan Levy, *God Bless You Real Good* (New York: Essandess Special Edition,
Simon & Schuster, 1967), pp. 54f.

[3]*Ibid.*

[4]Quoted in Glenn Daniels, *Billy Graham: The Man Who Walks with God* (New York: Warner Paperback Library, 1961), p. 27.

[5]Marshall Frady, *Billy Graham: A Parable of American Righteousness* (Boston: Little Brown, 1979), p. 513. Three earlier studies that put Graham in a more favorable light, and show his evolution, are John Pollock, *Billy Graham* (London: Hodder and Stoughton, 1966) Stanley High, *Billy Graham* (London: Kingswood, The World Work, 1957); and George Wilson, *Twenty Years Under God* (Minneapolis, World Wide Publishers, 1970).

[6]A full discussion of these matters can be found in Richard Quebedeaux, *By What Authority: The Rise of Personality Cults in American Christianity*. My own thoughts are summarized in *Seven Pillars of Popular Culture*.

A Man, A Prophet, A Dream

Dean Fadely and Ronald Greene

Dr. Martin Luther King, Jr. was a man with a dream—a dream which was deeply rooted in the American dream that all people are created equal, that they are endowed by their creator with certain unalienable rights.

The events which took place during the week of January 17-January 24, 1987, in the suburban Atlanta town of Cumming located in the red-clay hills of Forsyth County, Georgia, refocused this nation's attention on Dr. King's dream. A few dozen, non violent, civil rights marchers led by former King aide and current Atlanta city council member, Rev. Hosea Williams, were attacked by members of the Ku Klux Klan and Klan sympathizers. In a dramatic reversal from the way events would have taken place three decades ago, police arrested the attackers and protected the civil rights marchers. One week later an estimated 25,000 civil rights marchers defended by more than 3,000 National Guard, State, and local police replicated the march. The Mayor of Atlanta, Andrew Young, described the events surrounding this "March for Brotherhood" as follows: "In the 60's we were marching against state-sponsored racism. Here today, we are joined by our senators and protected by our governor."

Thus, the three decades between the 1950's and the 1980's reflect monumental changes—especially the changes in racial attitudes as advocated by Dr. Martin Luther King, Jr. These changes are, by definition, in keeping with the purpose of advocacy.

The purpose of advocacy is to effect change; this change may be as profound and sweeping as the change in ideology seen in the Soviet Union at the time of the Russian Revolution or in post W.W. I Germany; or, the change may be as seemingly simple as the purchase of a new necktie. However, no matter how complex or simple the change, all advocacy has certain commonalities. Probably no one reading this essay has had the following experience: you awaken one morning, get dressed, and drive to work. On the way, you pass a dentist's office. Suddenly, you say to yourself, "I think I'll go in and have two or three preventative fillings and maybe a root canal or two." To the contrary, most people have to be convinced that they need dental work done before they will consider fillings, root canals, and other dental procedures. Consider another hypothetical situation which will probably never happen: you are driving by an Episcopal church. Suddenly, and without warning, you decide, "I'm tired of being a Southern Baptist, and I didn't especially care for Jerry Falwell's last televised sermon anyway. I think I'll become an Episcopalian." For this type of change to occur, there needs to be a reason. Rational individuals do not institute change solely for the sake of change, without any reason to do so.

As long as people are satisfied with their lot in life, including the car they drive, the church they attend, the state of their teeth, the clothes they wear, or the job they hold, they are reasonably content to keep things as they are. *Things as they are*, this is an important phrase to remember. In the theory of argumentation the term *status quo* is used. *Status quo* is a Latin phrase which literally means state in which. In translation, the term means things as they are, the present system, or the existing state of affairs. Thus, if you drive a 1975 Monza with a four cylinder aluminum engine, that is the *status quo* for you in terms of automobiles. If you are a member of the Southern Baptist Church, that is the *status quo* for you in terms of religious affiliation.

Normally, a rational individual does not deliberately change his or her *status quo* without a reason. As long as the present system is satisfactory, there is a tendency to want to maintain it as is. In the theory of argumentation this concept is known as presumption, and it will be the subject of subsequent discussion.

Sometimes, it is easy for an advocate to adduce reasons which will make the auditor(s) want to change. For example, I can become convinced that a change of personal cars is in order merely by looking at the pictures of the newest models of the Mercedes-Benz 560 which the Mercedes advocates, in this case the manufacturers, have so thoughtfully arranged to have placed in the magazine which I am reading. Sometimes it is easy for another advocate, or the auditor, to refute the reasons which have been given for changing the *status quo*. For me, a trip to the local Mercedes-Benz dealer and a glance at the price of a 560 SL is usually sufficient. More often, though, it is not easy for the advocate to persuade his or her auditor(s) to change, or to accept change, even when it is in their best interest to do so. Thus, the study of advocacy arose in response to the perceived need to know why people want to change and how it is possible to persuade them to do so.

For change to eventuate, a particular process must take place, a process which can be seen in the following model of ideological and social change:

INVENTION

COMMUNICATION

ADVOCATION

Motivate
Reinforce
Actuate

ADOPTION	OR	REJECTION
(Presumption is overcome.		(For a variety of reasons,
The *status quo* is indicted.		the proposal the advocate
The proposal the advocate		espouses is not accepted.
espouses is accepted.		Change does not occur.)
Change occurs.)		

At the invention stage, the results of a new idea come to fruition. These results may be a new invention, for example, a new form of transportation, an improvement of an old invention, as in the new models of automobiles, or even a new ideology. No matter what the particulars, something new and different is conceived, and this idea or invention may be the work of many, few, or even a single individual.

The next step of the process is the communication of the new idea or invention among individuals. Many of these individuals will become advocates for this new idea or invention. In this third stage, the advocate(s) will try to convince others to accept or adopt the new idea or invention. Some people will be persuaded; adoption will take place, and change will occur. Other people will not be persuaded. They will reject the new idea or invention and, thus, change will not occur (stage 4).

Russel R. Windes and Arthur Hastings have summarized the role of the advocate who is trying to actuate auditors thereby causing them to accept an ideological or social change. They write of a proposition of action* in which:

...the advocate who upholds the proposition is calling for a change in behavior toward a specific policy, a specific way of meeting a problem. He calls for a new approach, a new program, policy, plan or proposal to meet needs not being adequately met under

*Most authorities refer to this type of debate proposition as a proposition of policy.

the status quo. Before he can displace presumption and achieve acceptance of his proposal, he must discharge certain obligations. He must present the problem which culminated with the proposition; he must demonstrate that the problems associated with the status quo are indeed serious, so serious in fact, that the consequences cannot be tolerated, or should not be. He should in many cases show that the consequences affect large numbers of people, i.e., the problem is widespread, hence is a public matter. He should be able to relate the consequences of the problem to valid causes, to identify those causes clearly, and to associate them as an integral part of the status quo. He should demonstrate that the problem is so related to the current basic theories and ideologies that its solution can come only through broad conceptual changes in both ideology and theory. He must then present a proposal which, through attacking the causes of the problem, will thereby eliminate the unwanted present consequences, producing results that are wanted.[1]

All of the above duties are obligations of the advocate of a policy change. Similar duties confront the advocate who would persuade auditors to change their value systems. In both situations the advocate is involved in trying to effect change.

Dr. Martin Luther King, Jr. was an advocate who sought to change the value systems of many of those with whom he communicated. He also wanted to change policies—policies which permitted and even encouraged racial discrimination. King wanted to change these policies and the value systems which undergirded them because he was a man with a dream, a dream in which he saw his people freed from the "binding manacles of segregation and the chains of discrimination."[2]

As he battled to fulfill his dream, Dr. King was pitted against the forces of segregation and discrimination—forces which were, all too frequently, part of the *status quo*. Therefore, King often had to argue his case from the position of the advocate of change. As such, he did not have the benefit of the presumption which is usually accorded to the *status quo*. King was, in short, a non-presumptive advocate and, as such diverse theoreticians as Beale, Minnick, Perelman, Warnick, and Whately[3] have indicated, a major task of the non-presumptive rhetor is to gain presumption, thereby shifting the burden of proof to the opposition.

Dr. King sought to effect this shift in the burden of proof by appealing to the values which he perceived to be the most important to his auditors, i.e., through the use of hierarchies of values. For example, Dr. Martin Luther King, Jr. and his colleagues believed that the segregated public bus system which existed in Montgomery, Alabama, and throughout the South before and during the early 1950s, was repugnant. Dr. King approached the officials in charge of the public transportation system and, essentially, spoke to them as follows: "You are making black people sit or stand in the back of buses in order to allow white people to always have a seat. This is not right." The officials, in effect, replied" "Yes, we make blacks give up their seats in the buses to whites. We do this because it is the law in the State of Alabama. We believe that the law is fair; we like it, and we intend to abide by it." Dr. King then replied, "'We believe that any law which forces one race to be subservient to another race is an unjust law and should be changed. However, what is more important to you, making black people give up their seats to white people or making the money necessary to pay your salary and keep the buses in operation?" Thus began the famous Montgomery, Alabama, bus boycott. The battle lines were drawn; the hierarchies of values were established. Eventually, white profit motive was to prevail over white prejudice. Dr. King and his followers were able to convince the powers that be that by giving up segregated public buses, they could attain a value evidently more important to them, $ $ $. Furthermore, since blacks constituted a mainstay of the ridership of the Montgomery Transit Authority, black business was a *sine qua non* for profit.

Montgomery was not an isolated example: In order to persuade, Martin Luther King consistently appealed to value hierarchies. At the top of his value system was the love of God, or as King referred to this type of love in Greek, *agape*. The next level was the love between men, represented by *philia* and *eros*. A set of morals could be established from this love. Morals were then utilized as the criteria for defining justice, and justice was the authority for laws.

Most of King's rhetoric attempted to take advantage of the fact that a religious hierarchy of values is predominant in the minds of most Americans. Wayne Minnick provides a list of "Religious values of contemporary Americans." Of this list, number seven states: "They tend to judge people and events moralistically."[4] So, in his famous treatise *Letter from Birmingham Jail*, King initiated his major arguments with the proposition "But more basically, I am in Birmingham because injustice is here."[5] Other strategies are interspersed within the text, but his basic argument is that the present injustice exists because of unjust laws. The laws are unjust because they are not moral. A moral law has to be based on love, and segregation is the negation of love as it is separation. Furthermore, there stands the strong implication that the negation of the love of man is also the negation of the love of God. King's immediate audience consisted of eight clergymen who had signed a letter denouncing his tactics. King started his letter by stating that he usually did not answer criticisms, but he would this time because these clergy were sincere men of good will. As a persuasive tactic, however, King had a much better approach. With clergy as his immediate audience,

King could utilize a value hierarchy of religious beliefs. He could gain support for his ideas by putting them on religious grounds. Furthermore, Dr. King could use this approach to avoid possible criticism which could reduce either his ethical appeal or credibility. As Minnick indicates, Americans in the sixties "think religion and politics should not be mixed; ministers should stay out of politics, and politicians out of religious matters."[6] King was obviously aware of this prevalent attitude and continuously explained his position as being in the tradition of prophets and Jesus Christ.

In contrast to King's Christian hierarchy of values exists a social hierarchy of means by which laws are established and justified. Of course, this system is based on voting for representatives who establish laws and regulations for the common good of the nation or state or municipality. In the *Letter from Birmingham Jail* King wisely avoided arguing on a political level, but elsewhere often did refer to the Constitution and to the doctrine of interposition and nullification which some states employed in an attempt to void the 1954 Supreme Court's decision of *Brown v. Board of Education.*[7] In his deliberative rhetoric Dr. King often pointed out that some states were ignoring, or even trying to counteract, federal law. However, the presumption of propositions of fact was not King's only rhetorical strategy.

In his book *Modern Dogma and the Rhetoric of Assent*, Wayne Booth discusses the fact-value split,[8] the notion that in terms of deliberation people will favor a fact over a value. He contends that as of at least seventy-five years ago the fact-value split has been a truism. In terms of deliberation people will favor a fact over a value. He makes two lists of things that fact-oriented people also accept. A few of the items under "scientismic" (fact) are: known facts, objectivity, reason, the provable, the knowable, empiricism. Under the heading "irrationalists" (value) he lists: values (the important), persons, faith, mind, spirit, knowledge of the heart, wisdom, the prophet or seer. Although King, his movement, and philosophy fall into the latter list, he is careful to begin his propositions with information from the former—facts. Even when King was addressing a "receptive" audience, it must be remembered that he often carried a heavy burden of proof because he was advocating nonviolence that sometimes led to violence, led to civil disobedience, led to jail, and even went against the philosophy of the oldest and largest civil rights organization in the United States, the NAACP. Dr. King was, indeed, a non-presumptive rhetor. The philosophy of the NAACP was based on the premise that the plight of the Negro could best be solved through improved education, and the best method for achieving better education was through the legal system—the courts, litigation and the like. One of the main arguments used to discredit King was that his religious hierarchy of values begged the question. He understood the argument of the clergy in Birmingham when they stated:

We further strongly urge our own Negro community to withdraw support from these demonstrations, and to unite locally in working peacefully for a better Birmingham. When rights are consistently denied, a case should be pressed in the courts and in negotiations among local leaders, and not in the streets. We appeal to both our white and Negro citizenry to observe the principles of law and order and common sense.[9]

In terms of avoiding the fault of begging the question Perelman suggests the following:

Among the points of agreement from which the speaker draws the starting point for his discourse, it is important to distinguish those which bear upon reality (i.e., facts, truths, presumptions) from those which bear on the preferable (i.e., values, hierarchies, and loci of the preferable). Although language and common sense designate by the terms "facts" and "truths" objective elements which force themselves upon everyone, an analysis undertaken from an argumentative point of view does not allow us to neglect the attitude of the audience toward these "facts," unless we are prepared to commit a *petitio principii*.[10]

Very characteristic of King's rhetoric was the initiation of a proposition with a fact or truth, mediated with a transitional metaphor, and argued from a value stance. For example:

Five-score years ago, a great American, in whose symbolic shadow we stand today, signed the Emancipation Proclamation.

HISTORICAL FACT/TRUTH
This momentous decree came as a great beacon of light of hope to millions of Negro slaves who had been seared in the flames of withering injustice.

USE OF METAPHOR TO COMBINE FACT WITH VALUE
It came as a joyous daybreak to end the long night of captivity.

USE OF METAPHOR WITH SHIFT OF EMPHASIS TO VALUES
But one hundred years later, the Negro is still not free.

VALUE STATEMENT
One hundred years later, the life of the Negro is still sadly crippled by the manacles of segregation and the chains of discrimination.[11]

USE OF METAPHOR WITH EMPHASIS ON VALUE STATEMENT

When King presented this speech in Washington, D.C., he had a receptive, enthusiastic audience present so he did not have to prolong the factual part of his proposition before quickly moving into metaphor and values. In his *Letter from Birmingham Jail* he had, at least in large measure, an unfriendly and unenthusiastic audience. The critic can sense his delay. After a paragraph of friendly introduction, he begins:

I think I should indicate why I am here in Birmingham, since you have been influenced by the view which argues against "outsiders coming in." I have the honor of serving as president of the Southern Christian Leadership Conference, an organization operating in every southern state, with headquarters in Atlanta, Georgia. We have some eighty-five affiliated organizations across the South, and one of them is the Alabama Christian movement for Human Rights. Frequently we share staff, educational and financial resources with our affiliates. Several months ago the affiliate here in Birmingham asked us to be on call to engage in a nonviolent direct action program if such were deemed necessary. We readily consented, and when the hour came we lived up to our promise. So, I along with several members of my staff, am here because I was invited here. I am here because I have organizational ties here.

FACTUAL AND SLOW PACED
But more basically, I am in Birmingham because injustice is here.

FACT FOLLOWED BY VALUE STATEMENT
Just as the prophets of the eighth century B.C. left their villages and carried their "thus saith the Lord" far beyond the boundaries of their towns, and just as Paul left his village of Tarsus and carried the gospel of Jesus Christ to the far corners of the Greco-Roman world

FACT OR TRUTH
so I am compelled to carry the gospel of freedom beyond my own home town.[12]

VALUE STATEMENT
This latter statement asserts two propositions, being *compelled* by the precedent of the prophets and Paul and carrying the gospel of *freedom*. The technique of shifting from a fact or truth to a proposition involving a value judgment, although not unique to King, is an effective tactic which helps a rhetor to adjust his proposition to his audience. As a final example, the following is the opening proposition of a speech presented to a well-educated, mostly black, and agreeable audience. *The Philosophy of the Student Nonviolent Movement* was presented to the 1961 annual meeting of the Fellowship of the Concerned.

I have been asked to talk about the philosophy behind the student movement. There can be no gainsaying the fact that we confront a crisis in race relations in the United States.

FACTUAL AND TRUTH TO HIS AUDIENCE
The crisis in 1954 outlawing segregation in public schools has been precipitated on the one hand by the determined resistance of reactionary forces in the South to the Supreme Court's decision.

FACTUAL AND TRUTH TO HIS AUDIENCE
And we know that at times this resistance has risen to ominous proportions. At times we find the legislative halls of the South ringing loud with such words as "interposition" and "nullification."

FACT METAPHOR AND VALUE
And all these forces have developed into massive resistance. But we must also say that the crisis has been precipitated on the other hand by the determination of hundreds and thousands and millions of Negro people to achieve freedom and human dignity.

FACT BUT MOSTLY VALUE STATEMENTS
If the Negro stayed in his place and accepted discrimination and segregation, there would be no crisis.[13]

A PREDICTION WHICH INCLUDES A VALUE JUDGMENT

In his book *The Realm of Rhetoric* Perelman mentions that Descartes' *Discourse on Method* added the final rule, "To make so complete an enumeration of the links in an argument, and to pass them all so thoroughly under review, that I could be sure I had missed nothing." But Perelman argues that this is fine in mathematics but is rather daring when considering philosophy.[14] King is using rhetoric, not science, to demonstrate his philosophy. Even though King is often explicit and factual, his greatest ideas are held within the interrelated association of values.

Many of the ideas and values of King are found again and again in his various speeches and writing. These are just a few which can be found throughout his rhetoric:

1. Three kinds of love: *agape, eros, philia*;
2. There are just laws and unjust laws;
3. A law is just if it is moral; if it is not moral it is my duty to break it;
4. The necessity of civil disobedience;
5. People in power do not give up their privileges willingly;
6. That time will take care of things is a myth; time is neutral;
7. Hitler's laws were legal;
8. Means are important not ends because means become the ends;
9. Segregation is immoral, unjust and therefore not legal;
10. We must have faith in the future;

11. 1954 Supreme Court decision, separate is not equal or moral;
12. The American Dream is not over—in some respects it is just beginning;
13. "Let justice roll down the waters and righteousness like an ever flowing stream," Amos 5:24;
14. Democracy can only be achieved by voting;
15. Nonviolent direct action is necessary, moral, just, lawful.

One question often asked by critics is whether or not the rhetoric has achieved the effect intended—was it successful? When the components of the rhetorical process are complicated this question is difficult if not impossible to answer. Not only did the rhetoric of Dr. Martin Luther King, Jr. address a myriad of propositions of fact, value, and policy, it was directed toward a heterogeneous society. Dr. King had several levels of audience besides just the immediate and distant. One level included the ministers who provided religious leadership. An extension of this level was the faithful—the religious, church-going sector of our society. Another level included the political leaders and those in power who influenced others and were the primary law makers. Yet another level consisted of members of various civil rights groups who wanted to effect a change in the racial situation. A last group included those who were ignorant of, or who did not care about, the injuries the policy of segregation caused. All of these groups, along with others, were addressed by Dr. King in a widespread complex message which encompassed many kinds of arguments and analysis.

One evaluative dichotomy which is often mentioned in reference to Dr. King's rhetoric concerns his methods. It has been argued that these methods were effective in the South. There segregation laws were rescinded and the plight of blacks was improved. Outside of the South, it has been said, King's activities were largely ignored and often caused more harm than good. If history were to prove this assessment to be totally true it would, upon reflection, still indicate a successful rhetorical effect.

Despite this somewhat conservative perspective, however, the passing of time and the events of history appear to foster three conclusions: First, Dr. Martin Luther King, Jr. helped us to rediscover that we could apply religious values explicitly to our social structures in a forceful, dynamic way in order to effect profound changes in these structures. Second, his movement caused the tension needed to speed the process of changing our laws. The Civil Rights Act of 1964 and the Voting Rights Bill are but two examples. And finally, he demonstrated by words and actions that it could be considered sinful and socially destructive to carry passivity to the point of allowing hatred to overcome love. The societal changes thus produced have had a profound impact on all segments of America's population. However, this influence has been felt most greatly in the black community. Bayard Rustin described the progress thus engendered:

Immense gains have been made in the fight for black dignity, self-respect, and identity. Such largely cultural gains have had immense social, economic, and political consequences. To understand the great psychological distance traveled, one need only compare the mind-set of black Americans who marched on Washington in 1983 with that of their counterparts in the 1963 march on Washington, led by Martin Luther King, Jr. and A. Philip Randolph. The marchers of two decades ago came to Washington in a state of quiet anxiety, fearful of possible police reprisals. Last year's marchers, by contrast, were a far more confident lot, urging Jesse Jackson to "Run, Jesse, run."[15]

While Dr. Martin Luther King, Jr. did not live to see his dream fulfilled, his rhetoric did help, and is still helping, that dream to become a reality. As events from Montgomery, Alabama, in the early fifties to Cumming, Georgia, in the late eighties have demonstrated, values and their hierarchies have been changed. King fulfilled the first and most important task of the non-presumptive rhetor. Presumption has been shifted. The burden of proof is now on those who would oppose racial equality. In the last analysis, this shift in presumption may have been the most pronounced effect of Dr. King's rhetoric upon society as a whole.

Notes

[1]Russel R. Windes and Arthur Hastings, *Argumentation and Advocacy* (New York: Random House, 1965), p. 86.

[2]Arthur Smith and Stephen Robb, eds., *The Voice of Black Rhetoric* (Boston: Allyn and Bacon, Inc., 1971), pp. 184-188.

[3]Walter H. Beale, *Real Writing* (Dallas; Scott, Foresman and Company, 1982), pp. 90-105; Wayne C. Minnick, *The Art of Persuasion* (Boston: Houghton Mifflin, 1968);Chiam Perelman, *The Realm of Rhetoric* (Notre Dame: Univ. of Notre Dame Press, 1982), pp. 21-32;Barbara Warnick, "Arguing Value Propositions," *Journal of The American Forensic Association*, 18 (Fall, 1981), 109-19;Richard Whately, *Elements of Rhetoric* (Carbondale: Southern Illinois University Press, 1963).

[4]Minnick, pp. 218-220.

[5]Martin Luther King, Jr., *Why We Can't Wait* (New York: Harper & Row, 1963), pp. 77-100.

[6]Minnick, pp. 218-220.

[7]347 U.S. 493 (1954) and 349 U.S. 294 (1955).

[8]Wayne C. Booth, *Modern Dogma and the Rhetoric of Assent* (Notre Dame: Univ. of Notre Dame Press, 1974), pp. 12-19.

[9]Charles Muscatine and Marlene Griffith, *The Borzoi College Reader* (New York: Knopf, 1971), pp. 329-30.

[10]Perelman, p. 23.

[11]Smith and Robb, pp. 184-188.

[12]King, Jr., pp. 77-100. An unrevised version of the "Letter from Birmingham Jail" may be found in *The Borzoi College Reader* cited above, pp. 331-45.

[13]Philip S. Foner, ed., *The Voice of Black America* (New York: Simon and Schuster, 1972), pp. 943-53.

[14]Perelman, p. 150.

[15]Bayard Rustin, "Are Blacks Better Off Today," *The Atlantic* (October, 1984), p. 122.

Editor's note: Dr. Fadely was solely responsible for the first section of this essay including the model. The second section of the essay, which treats in greater detail the application of the model to Dr. King's rhetoric was a collaborative effort between both authors.

TV Preacher Jimmy Swaggart:
Why Does He Say Those
Awful Things About Catholics?

David A. Harvey

A recent issue of the *Catholic Twin Circle* national weekly magazine carried the headline on the cover: "Television Preacher Jimmy Swaggart: Why Does He Say those Awful Things About Catholics?" (Kurzweil, 1985). Swaggart's on-the-air behavior has frequently gotten him into trouble with critics both inside and outside the religious community. After he was welcomed to the White House during the 1984 presidential election, a WNBC-TV editorial in New York compared Swaggart to Jesse Jackson supporter Louis Farrakhan (who called Judaism a "gutter religion"). The editorialist condemned Swaggart for calling Roman Catholicism "superstition" and "heathenism" on the air, and called for President Reagan to be as courageous as Jesse Jackson and make a "forthright repudiation of a major supporter" (Kurzweil, 1985, p.3).

Swaggart has been so strident in his attacks on both Catholics and Jews that in 1984 several stations in Boston and Atlanta refused to sell him air time, including one station which was owned by the Christian Broadcasting Network. His statement that Mother Teresa of Calcutta is going to hell unless she has a born-again experience was severely criticized in the media, along with a show in October of 1983 in which he showed on the screen gruesome pictures of Auschwitz and other Nazi death camps while seeming to suggest that the extermination of six million Jews was the result of their failure to believe in Jesus Christ (see Newsweek, January 9, 1984, p. 65).

He has also been the subject of an hour-long PBS "Frontline" documentary, entitled "Give Me That Big Time Religion," which raised a number of critical questions about his preaching, his pulpit antics, and his business practices (Cornell, 1984).

Swaggart has also been the subject of criticism within his own Pentecostal movement. A recent issue of *Charisma*, the leading periodical among charismatics, (and the magazine which named Swaggart as the fourth most influential leader in the charismatic movement in the past decade), listed Swaggart's criticism of Catholics as one of the major controversies and conflicts within the movement during the past ten years.

Swaggart's criticism is not reserved just for Jews and Catholics. Few institutions and groups in American society escape Swaggart's homiletic wrath. While most of his criticisms point toward what he considers the insidious advance of secular humanism (the "new religion in America"), and its' ultimate result—a Communist America, Swaggart is frequently specific in his attacks. Illiteracy, abortion, pornography, AIDS, and other social ills are the result of this advancing secular humanist belief which is destroying our country. According to Swaggart, (in a recent television sermon entitled "If The Foundations Be Destroyed"), "the foundations of this nation are being eroded, weakened,—and unless there is a turnaround we will ultimately be destroyed. And if they are destroyed...all that we have will be totally lost-absolutely and completely—and we will experience a hell on earth."

This "destructive humanist belief" is propagated through the institutionalized groups and organizations in America. A brief survey of some of Swaggart's TV sermons provides a catalog of organizations and groups which are participating in this destruction. The Supreme Court has "bathed this nation in blood" by their decision to legalize abortion (Swaggart, "God's Message For These Last Days). The National Education Association has a "designed, perpetrated, instigated plan to design a system that will purposely turn out illiterates, so they can no longer read the Bible or anything else, so they can't think for themselves and will then be easy to herd into a socialistic type of government" (Swaggart, "If the Foundations Be Destroyed").

At times Swaggart will attack several groups with one issue. The news media, the intelligentsia, and environmentalists are several of his favorite targets.

I'm talking about people who fight to save endangered species—values are twisted and warped—vaunted news media and intelligentsia—all upset, trying to save some Tennessee Snail Darter, the California Buzzard, and a lizard in Arizona, and that's hypocritical. This demonic, devilish, bunch murders a million and one half babies every year in mothers wombs...(Swaggart, "God's Message For These Last Days").

In spite of the facts that Swaggart's criticisms may be dismissed as nonsense by many, and that his speaking in tongues and emotionally charged behavior may be considered odd, Swaggart is very successful. "Jimmy Swaggart Ministries" has become a world-wide multi-faceted enterprise. He claims to be watched by 150 million people each week in 116 countries, to feed over 204,000 children each month and support 490 missionaries, and that in the last two years over 900,000 letters have been received from people who said they have "received Christ" as a result of his telecast (*The Evangelist*, March, 1986, p. 30).

While Swaggart's statistics, especially those of viewership, are disputed by some (see Horsefield, 1984; Gerbner et al, 1984), the February 17, 1986 issue of *Time* magazine reports that his income is $140 million per year, that his show is aired in 197 markets, and that when he opened the Jimmy Swaggart Bible College in 1984 he received 18,000 applications for 400 openings (Ostling, 1986). Recent ratings surveys by Arbitron and Nielson have shown that Swaggart is the most watched weekly religious television show (see Horsefield, 1984, Gerbner et al, 1984, Ostling, 1986). The most recent survey shows that his program reaches 9.3 million household per month in the United States (Ostling, 1986, p. 67).

These facts raise several questions about Swaggart. Why would one whose organization is dependent on income generated by public exposure be so sectarian and say things and act in ways that are not generally expected on TV? *Time* alludes to this question: "Anyone who believes that TV has made the 'hot' Gospel hell-raisers obsolete has not seen one of Swaggart's sweating, mike-toting, Bible-waving, Devil-thrashing performances" (Ostling, 1986 p. 68). What purpose might Swaggart's public criticisms of institutionalized groups serve? Why is he so harsh in his televised sermons; why does he say those awful things about Catholics?

One possible answer to these questions is that these critical comments actually help Swaggart mobilize resources from people who watch his program and attend his crusades. A primary requirement for anyone who leads a collective movement is that he or she mobilize resources from constituents. Fireman and Gamson (1979) have suggested three requirements that collective leaders must fulfill to mobilize resources. They must (1) raise consciousness of shared interests, (2) provide opportunities for collective action, and (3) tap into feelings of solidarity and principles.

An analysis of Swaggart's rhetoric reveals how criticism helps to fulfill these three requirements. Even though these public criticisms may

Jimmy Swaggart.

Heirs-apparent of the Swaggart empire: son Donnie (already a TV star in his own right) wife and children. No effort is made to conceal their new affluence.

Royal succession: Father Jimmy Swaggart stands by his wife, and the anointed son stands by his.

involve significant risk for Swaggart by narrowing his base of support, paradoxically they also serve a necessary function in mobilizing support.

For Swaggart to mobilize his constituents to support his ministry and his cause, he must raise consciousness of shared interests. His criticisms play a strategic role in fulfilling this requirement.

The starting point of Swaggart's preaching is his view of the dangerous conditions of society, particularly American society. Society is on the brink of destruction, the institutions we have trusted have failed us, our children's futures are in imminent danger because of twisted values, and the country is closer than we think to becoming Communist, hence atheistic. These dangers have not arisen by chance, they are part of an insidious plot by leaders of the various institutions of American society to wipe out belief in God and the Bible and replace that belief with organized atheism, which will bring inevitable self-destruction. The further we get from God and the Bible, the more twisted values become, the closer we come to destruction and fulfillment of the plan of the anti-God humanists.

To create this reality of imminent danger, Swaggart resorts to harsh criticism of present conditions and the institutionalized powers "responsible" for those conditions.

The following excerpt from a Swaggart sermon will illustrate his use of criticism to raise consciousness of shared interests with his audience. The Sermon is entitled "The New Evangelists" which Swaggart defines as "media representatives," "the entertainment industry," and the "news gathering and news disseminating industry."

I want you to understand where these people are coming from. 93%—you see, the devil doesn't like his rot to be uncovered, he doesn't like the lid pulled off his garbage— 93% of media representatives do not attend church. 93% have no church affiliation. 85% of media representatives, these new evangelists, admit that they are liberals, a term synonymous with secular humanist, which is a term synonymous with atheist or agnostic.... Are these new evangelists successful at propagating their religion? I'll tell you how successful they are. Everyday in the United States, 365 days a year, 1,000 children, teenagers, attempt suicide.... The new evangelists, their new religion, secular humanism, to abolish God from our schools, our government, our homes, to abolish Christianity. What is the future? The die has been cast.

Swaggart's criticism of the media, or "new evangelists", is used to identify concerns that he shares with his audience. They don't want teenagers committing suicide because of the media, they do want the "devil's rot" exposed, and there is an implicit concern about these "new evangelists" who are "atheistic" being in a position of power in our society.

This type of message is neither new nor unique to Jimmy Swaggart. Other TV preachers such as Jerry Falwell and James Robison proclaim a similar interpretation of present conditions (see Hadden and Swann, 1981, Horsefield, 1984). This juxtaposition of seemingly dangerous current events and trends with the future of the nation and hence our children, has been seen as a source for making Jerry Falwell and the Moral Majority credible to people who disagree with Falwell theologically (Yankelovich, 1981). For Swaggart and other TV preachers, this message fulfills the requirement of raising consciousness of shared interests.

These criticisms reflect Swaggart's common interests with several different groups, foremost among whom are Pentecostals. Since their inception as a movement in the early nineteenth century Pentecostals have prided themselves on being different than the rest of society and being able to discern the "evil" in society (see Nichol, 1966, Synan, 1971). Their rejection of society, and being rejected by it are seen as marks of the true church. Church services that included displays of emotion, including such things as the "holy dance," the "holy laugh," being "slain in the Spirit" and speaking in tongues, were accepted as the norm for Christianity. "Pentecostals rejected society because they believed it to be corrupt, wicked, hostile, and hopelessly lost, while society rejected the pentecostals because it believed them to be insanely fanatical, self-righteous, doctrinally in error, and emotionally unstable" (Synan, 1971, p. 185).

Swaggart's roots are in the Pentecostal movement, particularly the Assembly of God denomination in the South. Even though he has become nationally known he has kept close ties to this fast-growing denomination, and has not deviated from traditional Pentecostal beliefs. The small Assembly of God church in the town of Ferriday, Louisiana, where Swaggart was "saved" and "baptized in the Holy Spirit" is included in a film clip shown at the beginning of most Swaggart telecasts. His city-wide crusades are still sponsored primarily by Assembly of God churches in the area. His denunciations of modern society serve to identify him with the contemporary Pentecostal movement, raise consciousness of shared interests, and thus ultimately aid in mobilizing resources from that group.

As Swaggart also needs to raise consciousness of shared interests with several other groups, he must deal with the tension of remaining faithful to Pentecostal beliefs while at the same time broadening his appeal to other groups. To do this Swaggart appeals to groups that share the Pentecostal suspicion of society, namely non-Pentecostal fundamentalists and those sympathetic to the cause of the "new right."

Fundamentalists who do not consider themselves Pentecostal comprise a significant collectivity that is sympathetic to Swaggart's crusade for fundamental conservative values. (see Hadden, 1980; Newsweek, Sept. 15, 1980, pps. 28-36). Swaggart's fears are their fears, and even though they may not agree with his speaking in tongues, his expose of the dangers of liberalism combined with his emphasis on born again Christianity is something they readily identify with.

Like other television preachers Swaggart has been able to skillfully combine conservative Christian beliefs with the New Right agenda (see Hadden, 1980; Yankelovich, 1981; Horsefield, 1984). Recent presidential elections have demonstrated that the New Right has a significant constituency, not all of whom identify with born-again Christianity. Swaggart's extreme criticisms of institutionalized groups and organizations serve to identify himself and those sympathetic to the New Right as having a common enemy, a common cause, and common concerns about the future.

A second requirement faced by one seeking to mobilize resources from a collectivity is that of providing opportunities for collective action. For Swaggart, who heads no political action committees and leads no grass-roots demonstrations in which his constituents may participate, and who generally restricts his own public activity to singing and preaching, this requirement could be particularly troublesome. Yet, his top-rated television audience size and "standing room only" crusade audiences are testimony to his ability to mobilize constituents.

Swaggart's invitation to collective action is an invitation to participate in the drama of redemption. Larson suggests that the success of motivating a collectivity to action is dependent on a leader's ability to create in the minds of the audience the sense of a momentous event, and to invite the audience to participate in the drama of that event (1983, p. 175). Swaggart mobilizes resources of several different groups by inviting viewers to participate in this drama of redemption.

This drama is played out in Swaggart's sermons by the pattern of harsh criticism which dramatizes society's guilt and need for purification and redemption, followed by highly emotional descriptions of what it's like to be redeemed.

This pattern may be seen in the following excerpt from Swaggart's sermon "If The Foundations Be Destroyed." He has been attacking secular humanism which he has described as "the most deadly, denigrating, damnable, dastardly thing that could ever come from the lips of man," and lists several characteristics.

It is self-authority, which means that man is his own authority an not accountable to any higher power. This self-sufficiency generates self-interest, self-gratification, self-indulgence, and self-righteousness. That's the reason this nation, part of it, despises Jimmy Swaggart maybe more than they despise anyone else is because I tell them in no uncertain terms, "sir, your self-righteousness is as filthy rags in the eyes of almighty God, you are a poor helpless sinner, you cannot save yourself, all of your good works cannot save yourself, the only way you'll ever be saved is to come to the foot of the cross and kneel at the feet of the world's redeemer and accept Jesus Christ as your own personal savior, and if you don't do it you're gonna die and go to Hell!

Constituents can participate symbolically through watching the drama played out before their eyes during Swaggart's services, and may participate tangibly through contributing to the organization of the one who is working to "bring purification."

For Swaggart to continue to buy television time, he must find a way to direct this participation into the tangible action of making financial contributions. To do this, Swaggart must convince constituents of the urgency of contributing to his organization. He must convince them that without support for his organization, principles that are important to his constituents and other collective goods may be in serious jeopardy.

Urgency is a function of necessity and opportunity (Fireman and Gamson, 1979, p. 27). Events that decrease the likelihood that constituents can realize their interests without collective action increase necessity for collective action. Resources can be mobilized if a collective leader can increase the perception that his organization plays a critical role in achieving group goals. There are several ways in which one may do this. Direct threats to specific group interests may be posed, trust in authorities may be undermined, and rival possibilities for collective action may be discredited.

Swaggart's criticism functions in all three ways to increase the necessity of contributing to his organization. The following excerpt from Swaggart's sermon "If the Foundations Be Destroyed" contains specific threats to group interests, undermines trust in auths of the Gospel, using the King James version of the Bible, as a text book to teach little Johnny...in the Word of Almighs of the Gospel, using the King James version of the Bible, as a text book to teach little Johnny...in the Word of Almighty God, and they got the greatest education the world has ever known.... The NEA designed to take over the American school system and has almost done it. A study of NEA records shows that it is not interested in education and that it is not interested in teachers.... The NEA has set out to make a socialist nation of this country....

In this quotation Swaggart presents a direct threat to specific interests of his followers—both the education of their children and the future of democracy are at stake. Further, he asserts that authorities cannot be trusted because they are part of the plot, and if someone is interested in the future of education in the country and in preserving the democracy it is futile to work through either the NEA or the government; Jimmy Swaggart is the one who "understands" what is happening and is mobilized to fight this "imminent destruction." Since Swaggart's charges and criticisms are more explicit than other television preachers, there may be an implicit message that Swaggart perceives the danger better than those preachers who are not so harsh, thus his rhetoric may increase the necessity of supporting Jimmy Swaggart Ministries over other ministries.

A third requirement for collective leaders is that they must tap into solidarity and principles to mobilize resources from collectivities effectively. Solidarity arises from factors that link members of groups together and may be described as "a sense of common identity, shared fate, and general commitment to defend the group (Fireman and Gamson, 1979, p. 21). Principles are rooted in individuals' interest in collective goods which they perceive the group deserves as a matter of justice, equity, or right.

One way that a collective leader may "tap into" solidarity is by appealing to group interests. Groups have interest in preserving or achieving collective goods. To mobilize resources from a group a leader needs to identify his or her program with a group's goals and design for living.

To appeal to principles a leader must approach constituents with "some vision of justice or equity with which they hope to raise some righteous anger" (Fireman and Gamson, 1979, p. 26). According to Fireman and Gamson, discontent must then be focused, the relationship between current events and abstract beliefs made clear, and the feelings of contention channeled by the resourceful leader. Ideological statements that express the collectivity's view of reality in a simplistic yet urgent manner are particularly beneficial. Issues and groups may be polarized, metaphoric language employed to raise and focus anger, and everyday events distorted, exaggerated, or placed in a new context, all to make plain the vision and reveal the imminent danger.

Swaggart's sermons are frequently punctuated with these appeals to solidarity and principle. They are usually framed in terms of conflict over symbols which reflect constituent's moral worth and claims to status, and as a fight for the ideals of the group (Oberschall, 1973).

Criticism of established groups in society is an indispensable tool used by Swaggart in establishing the nature and seriousness of this conflict. Because the conflict is seen as conflict over "indivisible goods" and "irreversible issues," the use of radical and harsh tactics (criticism) is justified.

Typical of the Swaggart appeal to solidarity and principle through the use of criticism is this quotation from his sermon, "If The Foundations Be Destroyed."

We're gonna turn it around, with God's help we're gonna turn it around. I want to serve notice on YOU—we Christians, born again, are declaring WAR! We are declaring war on the monkeys in our classrooms; we are declaring war upon the secular humanists; we are declaring war on the atheists and evolutionists; we are declaring war on the abortionists. We're bringing back the Bible to the United States of America, bringing back the Bible to the pulpits of our nation—one nation, under God, with freedom and justice for all—America—the land of the brave, the home of the free.

The notions of common identity and shared fate which appeal to solidarity are clearly evident in this quote. "We Christians" are going to war and are bringing the Bible back to the United States. "We" are going to fight to make this nation once again a nation "under God, with freedom and justice."

Swaggart appeals to principle by presenting a vision of a world that is not just and equitable for his constituents. Clearly he indicates that his constituents have suffered injustice—monkeys in their classrooms, secular humanists, evolutionists, atheists, and abortionists have been in power too long. The metaphoric war language, the idea of secular humanists, atheists, evolutionists, and abortionists allied against born-again Christians, the out of context picturing of Bibles being carried out of classrooms (and pulpits) and monkeys carried in, and the indivisible issues of patriotism, God, freedom, and justice, combine to make this a powerful appeal to constituents' principles.

Why does Jimmy Swaggart say those awful things about Catholics? One explanation is that his criticism is an integral part of a rhetorical strategy that enables him to mobilize resources from his constituents through raising consciousness of shared interests, providing opportunity for action, and tapping into feelings of solidarity and principles.

Bibliography

"A Tide Of Born-Again Voters." *Newsweek*. Sept. 15, 1980, pps. 28-36.

Armstrong, Ben. *The Electric Church*. Thomas Nelson Publishers, 1979.

Berckman, Edward M. "The Old Time Gospel Hour and the Fundamentalist Paradox." *The Christian Century*. 95, March, 29, 1978.

Boorstin, D.J. *The Image: A Guide Pseudo-Events in America*. New York: Atheneum. 1980.

Briggs, Kenneth. "Religious Media's Spreading Tentacles." *The Christian Century*. March 1, 1978.

_____. "The Electronic Church is Turning More People On." *The New York Times*. February 10, 1980.

Cornell, George W. "Documentary Takes A Look At TV Evangelist Swaggart." *Hazleton Standard-Speaker*. Feb. 11, 1984.

Doan. Michael. "The Electronic Church Spreads The Word." *U.S. News & World Report*. 19: 16, April 23, 1984.

Dollar, G. *A History of Fundamentalism in America*. Greenville, S.C.: Bob Jones University Press, 1973.

Fireman, Bruce and William A. Gamson. "Utilitarian Logic in the Resource Mobilization Perspective." In Zald, Mayer & John D. McCarthy (eds.), *The dynamics of Social Movements*. Cambridge, Mass.: Winthrop Press, 1979.

Gaddy, Gary D. & David Pritchard. "When Watching Religious TV is Like Attending Church." *Journal of Communication*. 35, 1985.

Gerbner, George, Larry Gross, Stewart Hoover, Michael Morgan, Nancy Signorelli, Harry E. Cotugno, and Robert Wuthnow. *Religion and Television*. A research report by the Annenberg School of Communications, Philadelphia: University of Pennsylvania, 1984.

Griffen, Leland M. "A Dramatistic Theory of the Rhetoric of Movements." In W.H. Rueckert (ed.), *Critical Responses to Kenneth Burke*. Minneapolis: University of Minnesota Press, 1969.

Hadden, Jeffrey K. "Soul-Saving Via Video." *The Christian Century*. May, 28, 1980.

Hadden, Jeffrey K. & Charles e. Swann. *Prime Time Preachers*. Reading, Massachusetts: Addison-Wesley Publishing Co. 1981.

Hoover, Stewart M. *The Electronic Giant*. Elgin, Illinois: The Brethren Press, 1982.

Horsefield, Peter G. *Religious Television: The American Experience*. New York: Longman, 1984.

_____. "Evangelism by Mail: Letters From Religious Broadcasters." *Journal of Communication*. 35, 1985.

Krohn, Franklin B. "The Sixty-Minute Commercial: Marketing Salvation." *The Humanist*. November/December 1980.

Kurzweil, John. "TV Preacher Jimmy Swaggart: Why Does He Say Those Awful Things About Catholics?" *Catholic Twin Circle*. 21:15, April, 14, 1985. pps 3-4, 8.

Larson, Charles U. *Persuasion*. Belmont, California: Wadsworth Publishing Co., 1983.

Mayer, Allan J. "A Tide of Born-Again Voters." *Newsweek*. 96, September 15, 1980.

McCarthy, John D. and Mayer N. Zald. *The Trend of Social Movement In America: Professionalization and Resource Mobilization*. Morristown, NJ: General Learning Press, 1973.

_____. "Resource Mobilization and Social Movements: A Partial Theory." *American Journal of Sociology*. 82, May, 1977.

McClendon, Paul I. "Selling the Gospel in Secular Markets." *Christianity Today*. 27, April 8, 1978.

"Memorandum." *The Evangelist*. March, 1986, p. 30.

Nichol, John Thomas. *Pentacostalism*. Harper and Row, 1966.

Oberschall, Anthony. *Social Conflicts and Social Movements*. New Jersey: Prentice Hall, 1973.

Ostling, Richard N. "Power, Glory-And Politics." *Time*. Feb. 17, 1986, pps. 62-69.

"Rough Edges." *Charisma*. August, 1985, p. 164.

Simons, Herbert W. "Requirements, Problems, and Strategies: A Theory of Persuasion For Social Movements." *Quarterly Journal of Speech*. LVI:1, February, 1970, pp. 1-11.

"Swaggart's One-Edged Sword." *Newsweek*. Jan. 9, 1984, p. 65.

Synan, Vinson. *The Holiness-Pentacostal Movement*. Wm. B. Eerdmans, 1971.

Turner, Ralph H., and Lewis M. Killian. *Collective Behavior*. 2nd ed. Englewood Cliffs, NJ: Prentice Hall, 1972.

Wilson, John. *Introduction to Social Movements*. New York: Basic Books, 1973.

Yankelovich, Daniel. "The Stepchildren of the Moral Majority." *Psychology Today*. November, 1981.

Zald, Mayer N. and John D. McCarthy (eds). *The Dynamics of Social Movements*. Cambridge Mass: Winthrop Publishers, 1979.

Why Jerry Falwell Killed the Moral Majority

Jeffrey K. Hadden, Anson Shupe, James Hawdon, Kenneth Martin

The emergence of the New Christian Right was one of the important stories of the 1980 presidential campaign, and for most of this decade, one man (Jerry Falwell) and his organization (the Moral Majority) monopolized media coverage of the growing political consciousness among conservative Christians.

After an initial period of awe over his apparent power, the mass media challenged his credibility and forecast his early demise from the national political scene. Despite repeated pronouncements of his demise, Falwell has refused to fade like a morning glory in the noon-day sun. Wherever he has gone, whatever he has done, he has commanded media attention with perhaps as much skill as anyone in America with the exception of the incumbent of the White House.

In January of 1986, without any advance warnings, Falwell boldly announced the creation of a new political arm which would go by the name of Liberty Federation. This new organization would *continue* the activities and interests of the Moral Majority, *while* also *pursuing a broader agenda*. "We want to continue to be the standard bearer for traditional American values. But it's time to broaden our horizons as well" Falwell said in a press announcement.

This dramatic move to kill the Moral Majority bore some resemblance to killing the goose that laid the golden egg. For over six years the name Moral Majority, as much as the brilliantly combative persona of Jerry Falwell, had served as a cannon and a lightning rod—both dishing it out and taking the heat. The name Moral Majority served also as a battle cry arousing conservative Christians and encouraging them to become involved in the political process. And it also sent tremors of fear and indignation into the hearts of millions of liberals.

How could Jerry Falwell decide to kill such an important symbol and communications instrument? From the beginning of high public visibility both Falwell and the Moral Majority have been controversial. Neither the man nor the organization has ever ranked very high in polls of public approval. In deciding to kill the name Moral Majority, Falwell apparently reasoned that he had reached a point where there was more to be gained by jettisoning the negative aspects of the name than in carrying the liabilities that had accrued to the name. That rationale seemed paramount in his press statement:

...the press for six years has bloodied and beaten the name, Moral Majority. There are a lot of people who will say yes to everything we are saying, but they dare not stand with us on particular policies for fear of getting tarred, hurt—that is, picking up baggage the media has dumped on us.

Hence, like a giant corporation deciding a new name would be good for business, Falwell said his political arm would henceforth be known as the Liberty Federation, not the Moral Majority.

Most commentators responded to Falwell's change of name with seeming indifference. Considering the tens of thousands of column inches of print on the Moral Majority over the previous six years, there was only brief notice and little analysis of the reasoning behind the change to Liberty Federation. "...[E]xtremism never does very well for very long in this country" wrote *Washington Post* columnist Mary McGrory. America had become fed-up with Falwell's "holier-than-thou" behavior. "[I]f Falwell wishes to realize his goal of making this a 'Christian nation,' " she stated with confidence, "it will not be enough to change the name of the Moral Majority to Liberty Federation. He must change his own."

Most of the media had long believed that Falwell and his band of "religious zealots" were neither moral nor a majority. So, without much pause for reflection or analysis, they seemed to accept the name change as an admission of failure and moved on to another story. Pat Robertson's interest in running for president quickly became the focal point of news about conservative religion and politics.

Before the Moral Majority is forgotten completely, or we witness its resurrection without remembering that it died, it is useful to examine more carefully Falwell's rationale for the name change.

The thesis we shall advance is that Falwell had very good reason to kill the Moral Majority, but that reason was not the one he advanced, i.e., unloading the negative baggage that had accrued as a result of so much tarring and feathering from the media. Contrary to the general media impression that the name change represented admission of failure, we argue that it was success that led to the slaying of the goose that laid the golden egg.

Our conclusions are reached through a circuitous route and are not without ambiguity and irony. The *circuitous route* takes us through the yellowing pages of back issues of the *Moral Majority Report,* the official news publication of the Moral Majority. They reveal secrets of suspected organizational impotence—unobtrusive measures as real as the dental records of a deceased mortal.

The *ambiguity* of the story is that we will never be able to assess empirically the degree to which the Moral Majority was responsible for stimulating political action by conservative Christians in America. One of the oldest propositions in sociological lore is that when people believe something to be real, it becomes real in its consequences. Notwithstanding considerable evidence of a gigantic hoax, the media and people from every walk of political life from the far right to the far left believed the Moral Majority to be a well organized and significant social movement organization. As a result of this widely held belief, the Moral Majority was significant. But there was scarcely any social movement organization there at all.

The *irony* of the story, hence, is that Jerry Falwell's requiem for the giant he slew was probably not very far from an accurate assessment:

"...we [the Moral Majority], more than any other organization in America, have been responsible for the conservative turn around in this country in the past six years."

ASSESSING THE MORAL MAJORITY'S STRENGTH:
A LITERATURE REVIEW

Assessing the real organizational strength of the Moral Majority has been a matter of interest to virtually everyone involved in understanding the political process in America. Ronald Reagan concluded early that Jerry Falwell had a significant following and he has acted accordingly during his presidency. Now, George Bush's advisors, as well as Republican operatives across the country, are debating the assets and liabilities of Falwell's support. Liberal Democrats have a serious interest in assessing whether the Moral Majority is really a threat to their value preferences and political power or, as many of them believe, merely a "paper tiger." Students of social movements too are interested in forecasting the strength and the potential of the conservative movement in America, and where the Moral Majority fits into this broader movement.

Social movement organizations typically provide little organizational data. What they do offer is likely to be self-serving and, thus, must be treated with caution. It is virtually a truism that SMOs systematically "fudge" organizational numbers to exaggerate their power. And since memberships, financial data, and other organizational records are not readily accessible for public inspection, SMOs typically utilize made-up statistics to create impressions of much greater organizational strength than they actually have. Few people have worked the magic of made-up organizational figures more skillfully than Jerry Falwell. (An insider joke among people who work for Falwell is that "Jerry never lies...he just remembers big.")

In the absence of reliable data, how can we assess the organizational strength of SMOs generally and the Moral Majority specifically? The answer is that we must rely on indirect measures. Two broad classes of data have been utilized to try to get a better picture of the size and strength of the Moral Majority.

The first class of data involves a variety of *indirect measures of support* for the Moral Majority. What do people think about the Moral Majority? Where is the general public viz the value preferences of the Moral Majority?

Studies which attempt to measure support for Falwell and the Moral Majority are fairly consistent in recording low rates of approval. A 1981 Gallup Poll found that 40% of the respondents of a national sample had heard of the Moral Majority while only 8% approved of the organization (Gallup Report, 1981: 60). In 1982, Gallup found that recognition of the Moral Majority had increased to 55% and approval had grown to 12%, with 5% expressing an interest in joining (Gallup Report, 1982: 170). But Gallup polling in subsequent years failed to reveal any appreciable increase in Moral Majority popularity.

In Dallas-Fort Worth, which Shupe and Stacey call the heart of the Bible-Belt, they found that only 16% expressed favorable attitudes toward the Moral Majority while 31% expressed hostile feelings toward the organization (1983). In Indiana, Johnson and Tamney conducted two separate studies in "Middletown" and support for the Moral Majority declined from a slim 16% in 1981 to 14% in 1982 (1983: xx; 1984: 189).

In a national study, Buell and Sigelman found about 3% outright support for the Moral Majority and another 6% were classified as sympathetic with the Moral Majority. In sharp contrast, fully two-thirds (69%) were either hostile or critical of the organization and their beliefs (1985: 431).

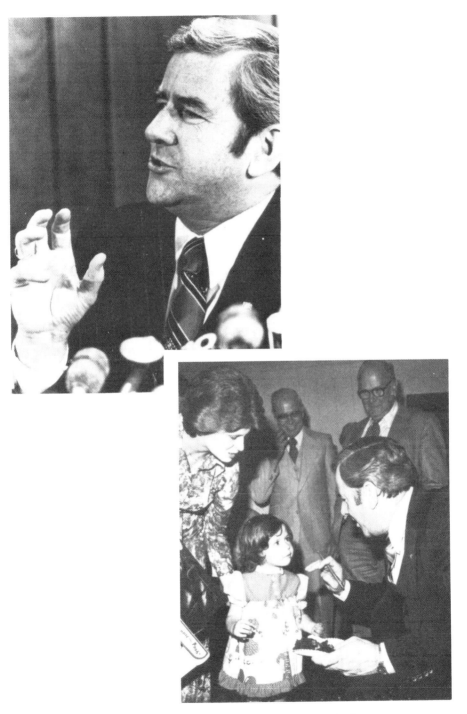

Televangelism is big business-
many cameras make light work.

On the other hand, studies which have attempted to estimate Moral Majority support by determining what proportion of the population support views consistent with the organization's position have produced much higher support. Analyzing *New York Times/CBS News* poll data, for example, Yankelovich (1981:5) concluded that 67 million Americans were potential Moral Majority supporters. And Simpson (1983: 188-190) analyzed NORC data and found 30% of the population were in agreement with the Moral Majority in disapproving homosexuality, the women's liberation movement, abortion, and federally mandated legislation restricting school prayer. On individual items, support for the Moral Majority position ran even higher.

This latter class of data supports Falwell's claim of having a significant proportion of the population with him on the issues but still unwilling to express sympathy for his organization. These data in conjunction with the low support obtained when the Moral Majority name is mentioned suggest Falwell may have acted with considerable wisdom in getting rid of the name—at least if his goal is to move toward "respectability" and broaden the base of organizational support.

A second broad class of data deal specifically with the actual *organization* of the Moral Majority. The number of studies in this second class is not large. Typically, they have utilized unobtrusive measures to glean insights about the size and character of the organization.

During the 1980 presidential campaign, Falwell claimed the Moral Majority had two to three million members. Hadden and Swann (1981: 137, 164-5) were able to pull together a number of organizational indicators from which they inferred that this size claim had to be significantly exaggerated. Among other things, they noted that the claimed circulation of the *Moral Majority Report* was only 482,000. Why don't all the members of the Moral Majority receive its official publication, they asked. They learned also from the Executive Director of the Washington state Moral Majority that his chapter had 12,000 members. The national office of Moral Majority confirmed that Washington state had the largest membership of any state. Simple arithmetic led to the conclusion that the total size of the national organization had to be much smaller than Falwell was boasting.

Probably the most perceptive glimpse into the organizational character of the Moral Majority was offered by Liebman (1983). From the onset, Falwell claimed that the Moral Majority represented a broad ecumenical base of Protestants, Catholics and Jews. Utilizing the directory of state chairman published in the *Moral Majority Report*, Liebman went to local telephone directories, and a variety of other resources, to see if this claim could be substantiated in terms of organizational leadership. He was able to identify *forty-five of the fifty state chairmen as Baptist ministers.* Furthermore, twenty-eight of them were affiliated with a small alliance of independent Baptists called the Bible Baptist Fellowship.

Liebman's data seriously challenged the claim of broad based ecumenicity. Furthermore, he uncovered an important clue as to how Falwell was able to put together a national organization so quickly. The Moral Majority merely, but ingeniously, linked an already existing national communications network of conservative ministers, spread its umbrella over them, and gave them a name. From its origin, the Moral Majority had a running start with an already existing nascent national federation along with an extensive array of mailing lists.

Utilizing existing networks and organizational structures has liabilities as well as assets. As Liebman notes:

while the availability of pre-existing networks lowers the cost of mobilization, social movements organizations may have to pay a stiff price when they incorporate previously organized constituencies (73).

One important liability for the Moral Majority was the necessity of structuring the organization so that state charters were quasi-autonomous. Falwell claimed that local autonomy was an asset, but the record suggests there were significant liabilities as well. There were several incidents where people far to the right of Falwell engaged in activities and made statements that were so outrageous that Falwell had to publicly repudiate or disassociate himself from them.

A more significant liability was the problem of motivating people, already highly successful in their own right, to organize their own time and projects in the name of the Moral Majority. From the beginning, the Board of Directors consisted of pastors of "super churches" and only one of these persons actively pursued projects in the name of the Moral Majority. The others basically "lent" their names and otherwise went about their own business.

Such liabilities do not necessarily preclude the development of a strong national organization, or coalition of loosely networked state organizations under a national umbrella. But this knowledge should serve as a warning that Falwell would likely encounter difficulties in building a solid grass-roots organization. In the absence of substantiated evidence, one should approach claims of organization success with some skepticism. Development is not likely to be easy, and it should not be assumed, simply on the basis of unsubstantiated claims, that these liabilities have been overcome.

Just how successful Falwell may have been in building a strong grass roots SMO has been the subject of much speculation and debate, but there has generally been an absence of systematic efforts to find indicators of organizational strength. This paper is offered as a modest effort to fill that gap.

CONTENT ANALYSIS OF MORAL MAJORITY REPORT

Statement of Assumptions and Research Methods. As noted in our literature review above, the popularity of an SMO or its leader(s) is not a very useful indicator of organizational strength. We argue that a more useful technique for assessing organizational strength is to examine its *activities.* What are an organization's goals and projects? Is there evidence to indicate that the organization is engaged in activities aimed at achieving its stated goals?

The *Moral Majority Report* is a monthly newspaper offered "at no cost as an extension of the Moral Majority Foundation" (11/85 masthead, pg 2). This is the only regularly scheduled publication of Moral Majority and, as such, offers the best possible public record of Moral Majority activities.

We do not assume that *MMR* reports all activities of the Moral Majority. Some activities, such as lobbying, may be more effective if they remain low-keyed or even private information. Similarly, active SMO leaders are often too busy engaging in movement activities to stop and provide a chronicle of what they do. Thus, we would expect some underreporting of organizational activity. But it is also reasonable to assume:

(1) that the national organization has an interest in promoting itself to its "members" and other readers of *MMR*;
(2) that significant activities, whether carried out by the national or state organizations, will not go unknown to the tabloid and, thus;
(3) most significant activities will be reported in the pages of *MMR*.

A corollary assumption is that the absence of *reports* of organizational activity can be interpreted as an indicator of the lack of organizational activities.

In order to assess the nature and magnitude of Moral Majority activities, we conducted a content analysis of all issues of the *MMR* for the calendar years of 1984 and 1985. The *Report* appears in tabloid newspaper form, typically 24 pages in length.

A typical issue of *MMR* features some topic of interest to the New Christian Right, e.g., pornography, homosexuality, abortion, school prayer, etc. In addition to this feature section, *MMR* carries columns of several conservative writers, news stories of interest to conservative Christians, an insert about Liberty University and some commercial advertising.

Another regular feature of the newspaper during the time period of our examination was called "Moral Majority Reports." This section included reports from the "National Officers" as well as "State-By-State" reports. This section seemed ideally suited for our efforts to chronicle the activities of the Moral Majority.

Before deciding to focus on the "Moral Majority Reports" section of the newspaper, however, we conducted a global survey of the entire content of the newspaper. For the two year period under investigation, we concluded that the pages of *MMR* provide no evidence of sustained ongoing activities or projects that can be uniquely attributed to the Moral Majority. We expected that the Moral Majority would have programatic activities dealing with each of the topics featured in the newspaper, but we found little news about Moral Majority *activities* per se that would document specific organizational activities.

With this global evidence, we turned to a systematic analysis of the section of the news tabloid entitled "Moral Majority Reports." A cursory examination of the reports of the National Leaders revealed evidence that they, as individuals, were engaged in various activities, speaking, lobbying, etc. But again we found an absence of specificity regarding *organizational activities.*

Hence, we decided to concentrate our analysis on the "State-By-State" reports. The Moral Majority claims to be a grass-roots network of local and state organizations. If the organization is functioning well at this level, the state reports should provide good evidence of the nature and extent of grass roots activities.

The unit of analysis for this investigation, thus, is the State-By-State reports. Our strategy for analysis is to record all *activities* reported. An activity was very broadly defined as any event (general or specific) reported in the State-By-State sub-section of the Moral Majority Reports. Each activity was classified in terms of *nature* of the activity and the *issue content* of the activities. *Nature* refers to what was done, e.g. demonstrating, registering voters, monitoring legislators, lobbying, etc. *Issue content* refers to the substantive matter of the activity, e.g., pornography, abortion, homosexuality, etc. In addition we coded a number of demographic variables such as state, region, who participated, how many, the time frame, the target group, etc.

RESULTS

Who Reported?—The Moral Majority claims chapters in all fifty states. Ten states (20%) submitted no report at all during the two year time period of 1984-1985 which we studied. Eleven state chapters (22%) submitted one report, fourteen (28%) reported twice, and fifteen (30%) reported more than twice. Overall, there were a total of 104 reports published, including the District of Columbia. That amounts to an average of one report per year per state for the two year period examined.

Falwell has claimed strong support for the Moral Majority in all states and regions of the country, but the presence and absence of reports by state suggests a *strong regional character.* More than half (54%) of all the reports came from the South, states considered to constitute the Bible Belt. Of the ten states that failed to report, all were outside the Bible Belt region. The Northeast industrial complex (New England and Middle Atlantic) accounted for only 11% of all reports.

The distinctively regional character of Moral Majority activity is further evidenced by the proportion of states within each region that reported. All but one Southern state reported (94%) while approximately one third of the states in the East and West never reported. Furthermore, 81% of the Southern regional states reported more than once while only 44% and 39% respectively of the Eastern and Western region states did so.

We also observed that states were much more likely to report in 1984 (78%) than in 1985 (38%). The higher rate of activity in 1984 can partially be accounted for by the fact that it was an election year. This fact, however, cannot account for a dramatic drop in all kinds of activities between 1984 and 1985. (We'll return to interpreting this statistic in our conclusions.)

Activities Reported. The forty states plus the District of Columbia reported a total of 244 activities. Leading the list of activities is "lobbying," 17% of all activities. This is followed closely by "voter registration" which comprises 16% of all activities. "Monitoring" constituted 11% of all activities, but seldom did we find evidence indicating how a situation was being monitored. This led us to suspect that "monitoring" might constitute a certain "fudge factor," i.e., something to report when nothing was otherwise happening. "Meetings" comprised 9% of all activities, "demonstrations" 8% and "rallies" made up 4%. We identified a total of eleven activities with four or more mentions.

Who are the actors? Thirty-eight percent of all activities reported are claimed solely as Moral Majority activities. Forty-two percent of the time, the writer explicitly indicates that the activity is being carried out by Moral Majority in cooperation with some other group. Rather frequently, 12% of the time, the person writing the report uses the first person singular to describe the activity, e.g., "I spoke," "I appeared on a TV program," etc. Eight percent of the time the actors are another group, or actors who are unspecified.

We think it significant that more than half of all activities reported are things that would usually be done by a single individual. In this context, we also find the large proportion of joint activities (42%) suggestive of a broad class of MM activities. If Jerry Falwell appears as a speaker at a rally or meeting, we suspect that activity would likely be considered a *joint* Moral Majority activity even though the MM may not have been involved in organization and management of the meeting.

Time frame for activity. The time frame for which activities were reported also proved to be quite revealing. Of the 244 activities recorded, 105, or 43%, were identified in the *future tense*. That is to say, nearly half of the time the authors of the state reports are writing about things they plan to do, rather than things they have done or are doing. For the future tense activities reported in 1984, we attempted to follow up and see if the author later reported that the activity had happened. This involved a total of 76 projected activities. Of this group, we could not positively confirm that any of these projected activities actually happened.

Activity Content. What were the substantive issues which the Moral Majority activities addressed? In our coding we had some difficulty differentiating between *type of activity* and *activity content.* This was particularly apparent with two general categories of activities—election related tasks and "organizational maintenance." And these two issues topped our list of recorded activity content. More than a quarter of all activities (28%) dealt with election related matters. Matters pertaining to the organization of Moral Majority were the second most frequently recorded activity content, accounting for 14% of all activities. Together, they account for 42% of all activity content.

Part of our difficulty results from certain conceptual ambiguities that arise in differentiating between "type" and "content" of activity. But it is also evident that many of the reports simply do not report a substantive content. We clearly had a coding bias that was evident only after we completed the task. In the absence of content, we were prone to record type of activity as a substitute for content.

If we eliminate the election and organizational maintenance activities from consideration, we have a total of 147 coded substantive issues. Topping the list of concerns are issues relating to education with a total of 26% of all the contents recorded. The substance of the education mentions breaks down almost equally between matters relating to private and public schools. This is followed by abortion which constitutes 22% of all mentions and pornography with 18% of the mentions. Other issues include homosexuality (9%), drinking (5%), and church and state issues (5%). Other issues receiving less than 5% mention included patriotism, defense, ERA and family.

ASSESSING THE IMPLICATIONS OF THE DATA

One of the rationales Jerry Falwell offered for creating the Liberty Federation was that he wanted to broaden the base of issues which he addressed. Those who have listened to Falwell over the past half-dozen years probably feel that he has never seemed constrained when it comes to speaking out on matters pertaining to national defense and foreign policy.

But the data here show that to the extent that the Moral Majority has been addressing issues, they have focused extensively on matters of personal morality to the exclusion of social-structural issues. Developing concern for this broader range of issues among his followers would seem to require new organizational and educational initiatives. In this context, Falwell's bold initiative in giving the Moral Majority the axe takes on new meaning.

The creation of a new organization with a new image and a broader mission can be seen both as an initiative to rid himself of the negative sentiments that have accrued to the name Moral Majority as well as an effort to form a new conservative Christian alliance that he could move beyond the issues of personal morality.

Contrary to the old adage that data speak for themselves, the data we have extracted from the *Moral Majority Report* don't make much sense at all except as they are interpreted. First and foremost, we think the data here amassed point to the absence of a flourishing grass-roots organizational structure.

If there were a significant grass-roots organizational structure out across America, there would be abundant evidence of this in the form of reports of projects and activities. What we find, rather, is something more nearly approaching a facade. The state activity reports represent a form of impression management. The Editor of *MMR* found it increasingly difficult to maintain the facade because State Chairmen, who weren't doing much, were increasingly unwilling to cooperate in providing accounts which revealed how little they were actually doing.

The Moral Majority really was a goose with a golden egg. Falwell chose to use the glitter of the egg to attract the attention of the media and thereby promote his cause in the press rather than investing the egg in building grass-roots organization clout. Perhaps, from the beginning, Falwell was content to sound the trumpet calling evangelical Christians to action. It may never have been his goal to build a grass-roots structure. Or, perhaps he didn't understand that grass-roots organizations don't just happen—they must be staffed and built with the same discipline that goes into building any other effective organization.

Whatever may have been Falwell's intentions, he has served well the conservative Christian movement in America by raising consciousness and giving millions hope that their vision of America might be restored. He has masterfully created awareness of issues and ignited fires of hope.

Falwell has criss-crossed the country delivering hundreds of speeches and sermons which have aroused fundamentalists Christians. He has also quite self-consciously done combat with the press and with a select groups of liberals in America—e.g., Norman Lear, Ted Kennedy, Walter Mondale, Phil Donahue, etc. By arousing their wrath, he has brought attention to the conservative Christian movement. The hostility exhibited by liberals has served to move conservative Christians closer toward mobilization even though they may not particularly like Falwell.

If Falwell has made one strategic error, it is his incessant bragging about his millions of followers and herculean accomplishments. For the most part, the press has been amazingly uncritical of him, seldom submitting his made-up statistics to careful scrutiny. Herein, we find the horns of the dilemma which led him to slay the golden goose.

The Moral Majority was primarily an organization for grabbing media attention, built and supported by direct-mail technology. As such, it was increasingly in the precarious position of having the press scrutinize Falwell's boastful claims. Like the final revealing of the Wizard of Oz, Falwell has been ever vulnerable to the likelihood that Dorothy and her trio of companions on the Yellow Brick Road would one day step around behind the curtain to discover that the Great Oz's powers were largely a facade—more amplified voice and lightening machine than substance. That is always the risk when a social movement is predicated too closely on media imagery.

During the summer of 1985 Falwell lost his two vice presidents who had been the backbone of the Moral Majority since its founding. Cal Thomas, the quick-witted, sharp-tongued VP for Communications, decided to stride out on his own as a syndicated columnist and free-lance journalist, and Ron Godwin, MM's Executive VP, was seduced by big bucks to become a VP with the *Washington Times*. These near simultaneous developments provided Falwell with an opportunity to slip out from under the weight of his shaky Moral Majority edifice.

Charles Judd, a former national GOP fund-raiser who was hired by Falwell in April 1984 was promoted to head the organization. Judd's goal, with Falwell's blessing, was to engage in building the grass-roots organization that had not previously been accomplished. In November Judd claimed that the Moral Majority was now "a lot more substance than hype." In contrast to the Falwell model, Judd claimed "...our purpose is not to be a lightning rod. Our purpose is to mobilize the conservative. We don't need to be that visible to be effective."

These events, thus, set the stage for Falwell to climb out from under the Moral Majority. It had served its purpose, and the purpose of the New Christian Right, well. But it had run its course. Falwell himself had established sufficient national and international visibility and didn't need the organization to promote himself. In fact, as the data we have here reviewed suggests, Falwell's own image, over the long haul, might well be improved by killing the Moral Majority.

Thus in January 1986 did Jerry Falwell announce the passing of the Moral Majority and the birth of Liberty Federation.

There are lots of possible explanations for these developments. We've argued that it was success and not capitulation to the pressures of negative criticism that led Jerry Falwell to kill the Moral Majority. Like a lot of other decisions he has made, he saw a window of opportunity and went with it.

There are other factors that may also have contributed to the decision. Falwell is committed to building Liberty University into a class institution for the higher education of conservative Christians. His announced goal of 50,000 students may be another one of his whopping made-up statistics.

Falwell has also recently purchased a cable television network. He began feeding the *Old-Time Gospel Hour* onto the cable system via satellite in 1986, and has plans to begin regular extended broadcasting in 1987. In addition to broadcasting a lot of live events from Liberty University, Falwell will host a daily talk-show with lines open to the audience. Even some of his closest friends and associates don't think he has a chance of building a network that can compete with Pat

Robertson's or Jim Bakker's networks. But they also note that they would never have dreamed that he could have built a university with 6,500 students and with the quality of Liberty University in less than a decade.

Between the development of Liberty University and the Liberty Broadcasting Network, Falwell has two good reasons to settle down and stay home more. He also has reason to begin to soften the tongue that so infuriates liberal Americans. But those reasons may not prove to be compelling. Upon considered reflection, it may become evident that softening the tongue and cleaning up his image are not likely to increase the chances that liberals will send their kids to school in Lynchburg, nor their bucks to support his network.

Jerry Falwell got where he is today by his instincts, energy, wit, and sharp tongue. It seems pretty obvious that he rather likes the idea of everything in his organization coming up LIBERTY. But Falwell is also smart and pragmatic. If Liberty doesn't work for all occasions, he can try something else. And if Charlie Judd doesn't turn Liberty Federation into a grass-roots organization that is paying dividends he may be working for the Republican Party again, and we may well see that after the life and death of the Moral Majority comes its resurrection.

Electric Sisters

Richard G. Peterson

In response to *Time* magazine's feature article about televangelist Pat Robertson (Feb. 17, 1986), a man from Philadelphia wrote the editor, "Today's television preaching could be a curse or a blessing. The Almighty will find a way to reveal the false and the true prophets."

Whether you believe them to be false or true prophets, conservative Protestant televangelists have received a good measure of media exposure, especially since "Pearlygate"—the Jim Bakker-PTL scandal of money, sex and power—exploded in March 1987 onto the front pages and into evening news television. In *Charisma* magazine (Jan. 1986) Richard Lovelace pointed out "a new determination among fundamentalists and Charismatics to make Christian values prevail in our society...gaining new territory for the Lord, with an increasingly strengthened Christian army." And when an expert such as sociologist Jeffrey Hadden predicts that the Christian right—powered by TV evangelism—"is destined to become the major social movement in America" during the late 20th century, certain individuals and groups become nervous. Groups like Americans United for Separation of Church and State, the American Civil Liberties Union, Norman Lear's People for the American Way, Planned Parenthood, the National Organization for Women (NOW), and authors such as Flo Conway and Jim Siegelman (*Holy Terror*). And, most recently, F.H. Knelman (*Reagan, God and the Bomb*).

But others such as Pastor Richard John Neuhaus, author of *The Naked Public Square*, don't believe religious conservatives wish to take over the country and establish a theocracy, but simply want a chance to debate their concerns in the public square. Neuhaus uses an analogy to illustrate his point: "And so the country cousins have shown up in force at the family picnic. They want a few rules changed right away. Other than that they promise to behave, provided we do not again try to exclude them from family deliberations."

116

Conservative Protestantism includes Pentecostals, Evangelicals and Fundamentalists, and the vast majority of religious radio programming and television is conservative in tone. (A 1984 University of Pennsylvania survey estimated that regular viewers of religious TV shows numbered 13.3 million. A 1985 Nielsen survey showed that 21% of the nation's TV households tune into Christian TV for at least six minutes in a week, and 40% for at least six minutes in a month—that comes to about 61 million Americans with at least minimal exposure.) Politically, the message on these broadcasts is pro-family and conservative, railing against secular humanism, feminism, pornography, gay rights, abortion and what they consider today's substandard public education. As a rule, Fundamentalists and Evangelicals share very similar beliefs and values, but the Evangelicals tolerate a broader range of Bible interpretation and cultural outlook. The dominant celebrity for Evangelicals is the Rev. Billy Graham, who more amicably coexists with liberals within mainline denominations than do his Fundamentalist cousins; the professorial Jerry Falwell has been called a Fundamentalist of "genial manner and granite opinions;" and the flamboyant, dynamic Jimmy Swaggart is a Pentecostal preacher and Gospel singer.

Many individuals are familiar with some of televangelism's top-rated figures like the aforementioned Swaggart and Falwell, as well as Robert Schuller, Oral Roberts and Jim Bakker. But normal observation and logic indicate that the women on "Pray TV," whether with their own ministries or comprising husband-and-wife teams, don't spring as readily to public memory—if at all. Yet these women are colorful, vibrant individuals in their own right, and most of them serve as practically indispensable ministry partners. They may be examined within the context of the resurgence of conservative Protestantism in this country. However, it must be noted that some experts believe this resurgence has peaked, and that the religious landscape is really more complex than we believe. While this paper will not investigate that particular issue, keep in mind that among scholars there are differences of opinion about the actual vitality of modern-day conservative Protestantism.

****

An examination of religion in America reveals a surprisingly extensive literature concerning women, some of whom have played pioneering roles, e.g., Mary Baker Eddy, who founded the Church of Christ, Scientist, in 1879; Mother Ann Lee, whose magnetic personality and appealing doctrine greatly influenced Shaker social organization;

and Alma White, who organized revival meetings, joined her Methodist minister husband in evangelizing and founded the Pillar of Fire church.

Yet female membership has comprised only a small "sorority" within the largely conservative electric church. But despite their small numbers, each woman reflects a particular background and style to form a colorful kaleidoscope of personalities. While they differ in spiritual method and approach, they *do* share an increasingly sophisticated use of media power to reach into millions of homes and change people's lives. The following are thumbnail sketches of some past and present "sisters of spirit." (Note: the two "New Ager's" are included for contrast, and should not be construed as conservative Protestants!)

Sister Aimee Semple McPherson (1890-1944). Aimee was a Canadian farm girl who journeyed from milkpail to pulpit, who mixed healing with high living and preaching with spectacular publicity. "Sister" Aimee, a Pentecostal, founded the International Church of the Foursquare Gospel in Los Angeles; she built the Angelus Temple, and became the first woman to broadcast a sermon over radio (San Francisco, 1922). And Angelus Temple's KFSG (Kall Four Square Gospel) became the first radio station in the country to be owned and operated by a church. "What an opportunity to spread the gospel!" Aimee wrote. "My soul was thrilled with the possibilities this media [sic] offered..."

The always imaginative Aimee heralded two "firsts" during the initial years of her radio ministry. During the summer she preached from Angelus Temple into tents that had been erected in the surrounding areas of Santa Anna, Santa Monica, Long Beach, Pasadena, Huntington Park, Alhambra and Venice. In each tent a congregation assembled and listened to entire Temple services, which were broadcast through a radio receiving set. Another first took place when members were received into the church by means of radio. Aimee would ask,

'Do you believe in the Inspiration of the Scripture? In the Virgin Birth? In the atonement?' The Temple audience gasped in amazement, then cheered loudly, when the answer [via radio] came back, 'I do!' from a chorus of voices.

This enthusiastic response came from a telephone installed at her elbow, amplified at KFSG, and broadcast into the Temple auditorium and out over radio to be heard thousands of miles away.

In March, 1944 (the twentieth anniversary of KFSG), Foursquare applications for FM and television licenses were at the office of the Federal Communications Commission. Aimee announced that suitable hilltop acreage for a television transmitter had been purchased. The church newspaper reported that "in the near future Sister McPherson, who

A photograph of Sister as she was alighting from the aeroplane in which she flew over the city as the guest of the Stout Air Lines.

Aimee Semple McPherson.

pioneered radio preaching, will pioneer a new field, that of presenting her famous illustrated sermons by the miracle of television."

But she was found dead on September 27, 1944—only 54 years old— stricken by a heart attack induced by an accidental overdose of sleeping tablets. Twelve days later the internationally famous evangelist was laid to rest in Los Angeles' famed Forest Lawn cemetery after spectacular funeral ceremonies, which reputedly cost $40,000.

Kathryn Kuhlman (1907-76). The "one-woman shrine of Lourdes" from Concordia, Missouri, was known for her healing services in the 1960s until her death. "The power of God is going through a sugar diabetic" she would suddenly cry, pointing out into the audience. "There is a cancer, and every bit of pain has left that body. Somebody with a hearing aid on, take it off. You can hear. Someone with a heart condition is being healed."

Kuhlman had dropped out of high school because she felt an urgent call to the ministry. She first took to itinerant preaching in Idaho— once, sleeping in a turkey house for lack of other accommodations— then for almost two decades crisscrossed the American Midwest. Her healing abilities came to light by accident, when a woman announced one night that she had been cured of a tumor during a previous Kuhlman sermon. So convinced was Kuhlman that her role was only that of an intermediary for the "H-o-o-o-ly Spirit"—hers was a very dramatic speaking voice—she had a recurring nightmare about coming out on stage one day and finding the chairs empty, her healing gift gone.

She ran the Kathryn Kuhlman Foundation (a charitable, non-profit organization) from a hotel suite in Pittsburgh, where she prepared radio and television shows; about 60 stations carried her 30-minute radio broadcasts, five days a week, throughout the United States, into Canada and in overseas broadcasts reaching much of Europe. At CBS Television City in Los Angeles, she prepared telecasts that were viewed on some 65 stations, including WOR-TV of New York; her program was on television—490 half-hour shows were televised—for ten years. Hers was ultimately a globular, interdenominational following of millions.

Once asked how effective her television ministry had been, she replied.

The response is great, but unlike most other religious telecasts because we do not offer any giveaways. People write in only because they are hungry for the Lord. Financially, the telecasts do not pay for themselves. The greatest combination is television and radio...together they form a combination that is unbeatable.

Photo courtesy of Kathryn Kuhlman Foundation.

Evangelist Kuhlman was tall, slender and wore her auburn hair in a 1945 Shirley Temple style of long curls with a part in the middle. One observer described her as "a striking figure in a long, fleecy white dress with huge, billowy sleeves. . . her radiant smile and cheerful greeting cast their magic so quickly that the congregation was almost immediately on its feet, greeting her with thunderous applause." A reporter for a Pittsburgh newspaper thought Kuhlman appeared neither saintly nor spiritual, but was "supercharged with electric confidence and all the natural chutzpah-gusto of a whole slew of cheerleaders."

For more than 25 years Kuhlman held healing sessions throughout the country, prompting "miracles" that she attributed to God and that skeptics called psychosomatic. Her style was folksy and friendly, and as she touched the faces of those who reported healings, most would collapse "under the power of the Holy Spirit" into the arms of waiting aides.

Once, when asked about her healing powers, Kuhlman plaintively answered, "The Holy Spirit, people, oh, I'm so sold on the Holy Spirit. Don't you *understand?* Without the Holy Spirit I'm sunk, I haven't a crutch, I haven't anything to lean on."

Terry Cole-Whittaker. Known to devotees as just "Terry," this attractive, blonde, Southern Californian joyfully extolled fulfillment and wealth—material as well as spiritual. In a few short years, she had metamorphosed a sleepily La Jolla (San Diego) congregation into a swiftly rising star in the electric church firmament.

Ordained by the Church of Religious Science in 1975, Cole-Whittaker launched her first television program, called "With Love, Reverend Terry," in January 1979. Described as the woman who brought glamour back into religion, she used her post-college theatrical training and motivational speaking skills to full advantage. She appeared on dozens of radio programs, local and national talk shows (Merv Griffin, Phil Donahue) and in numerous print articles/interviews to promote her ministry and two best-selling books. Gavin MacLeod (the "Love Boat" captain) was one of her celebrity admirers as well as Linda Gray, Lily Tomlin, Eydie Gorme and Clint Eastwood.

Cole-Whittaker's teachings—often scored by Fundamentalists—contained a core of Christianity and Ernest Holmes' Science of Mind, with accretions of est, metaphysics, Eastern philosophy, humanistic psychology, Gnosticism and *A Course in Miracles*; one of her key postulates was "Prosperity and happiness are your divine right." Since evangelism is understood to mean proclaiming solely the gospel of Jesus

Terry Cole-Whittaker.

Terry Cole-Whittaker.

Christ and thereby evoking commitments to him, Cole-Whittaker was not precisely an "evangelist." Her theological eclecticism and open-minded willingness to use "whatever works" (spiritually) did not endear her to orthodox Christians.

At her ministry's zenith, the television program aired in 15 markets (primarily in the West but also on New York's "super station," WOR-TV). Her fourth husband, Leonardo, who was a minister in the Terry Cole-Whittaker Ministries and its administrative leader for 18 months, initiated a brief foray into radio that included a Spanish-speaking program. However, the radio ministry was discontinued after their divorce in 1984. Leonardo left to become rector of The Church of St. John the Evangelist in San Diego.

Cole-Whittaker was very comfortable in front of the camera and, her style was exhuberant, warm, just-plain-folks—with a disarming honesty. She termed her religious calling as a Divine Experiment and described herself as "a spokesman for the spirituality of the new age. I am not a Bible-thumper." However, as her fame grew, Cole-Whittaker became increasingly irritated with the accompanying publicity. Stories about her romantic life began appearing in the tabloids and strangers began knocking on her door. She complained, "You become public property and if people want to put a telescopic lens into your bathroom, they think they have the right."

In March 1985 she walked away from her pulpit, claiming a need for long-term introspection. Also, her organization had become unmanageable and burdened with a spiraling debt of $700,000. Cole-Whittaker attributed the latter to her loss of control of church finances and too rapid an expansion program. Considering that television evangelism is an enormously expensive proposition—the Jimmy Swaggart ministry was about $10,000,000 in arrears at one time—most likely programming costs made up a sizeable proportion of the debt.

Later, she continued for a while on television in Los Angeles, San Francisco and San Diego, "to support each of you who desires to receive a message of love, happiness, peace, unlimitedness and personal value." The programs were finally discontinued, and she created Adventures in Enlightenment, a foundation that promotes her books, speaking engagements, cassette teaching tapes and spiritual retreats to Big Sur, Hawaii, Australia, New Zealand and Fiji. Her latest book describes the lessons and challenges along Cole-Whittaker's "inner journey." And anyone who knows the irrepressible Reverend Terry doesn't discount the possibility of her getting back into television.

Marilyn Hickey. "And believe me, I didn't need any pictures to communicate to me the mass suffering and hunger that exist there [Ethopia]. I've been there [three times]. I've seen with my own eyes the tears of a mother as she had to part with her dead baby. I've looked into the eyes of death itself."

Marilyn Hickey discovered that her calling from God to "Feed my sheep" was not limited to spiritual meals alone, but also included physical food. Her Denver-based ministry has a strong humanitarian thrust: sending tons of bulgur wheat to Haiti and powdered milk to the Philippines; launching a "Fill the Ship" project in which a 500-ton cargo ship was used to transport food shipments to needy areas abroad; and periodically smuggling Bibles into the Soviet Union ("thus helping to ease the tremendous famine of God's Word in their land"), and more Bibles into Ethiopia, Lebanon, Poland and South Africa—a total of over 72,000 Bibles since 1983.

Called "the people's theologian" because of her practical application of the scriptures, Hickey is an average-looking woman with a conservative, low-key manner that is deceiving: she is iron-willed and operates a very professional, energetic, international ministry. She claims to have spent over 19 years in intensive study of the Bible, and uses Isaiah 11:9 as her ministry's cornerstone: "For the earth shall be full of the knowledge of the Lord as the waters cover the sea."

Hickey is a Texan who spent many years in Pennsylvania before

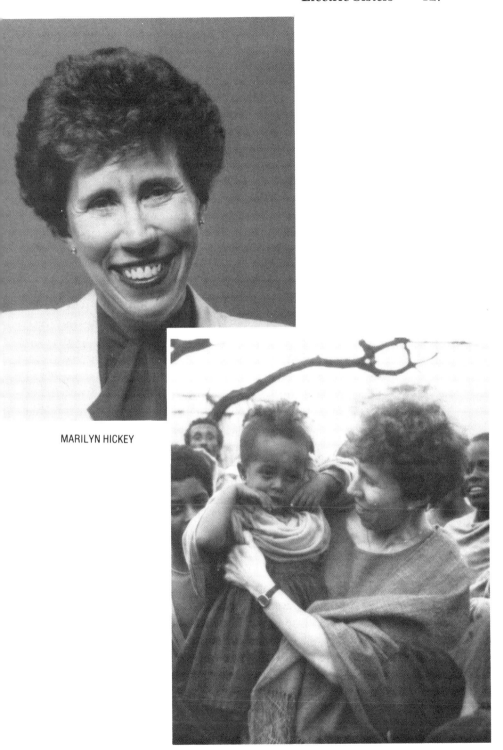

MARILYN HICKEY

MARILYN HICKEY
on a recent trip to Ethiopia

later moving to Denver. She earned a degree in foreign languages from the University of Northern Colorado. Being a pastor's wife, she initially felt her main ministry was to assist her husband, Wallace. But one day, while meditating on the Bible, she felt God call her to "cover the earth with His Word." It has been full steam ahead ever since.

Her monthly teaching magazine, *Outpouring*, is circulated to over 100,000 homes; she has authored over 30 books and booklets and produced countless teaching tapes and over ten video Bible teaching series. Her Marilyn Hickey Training Center is a two-year comprehensive Bible school, which is housed in Wallace Hickey's church (called Happy Church and described in their pamphlet as a "turned on" Charismatic body). Says Hickey, "Many seminaries have poisoned their students with humanism and with every type of false doctrine and wrong teaching. We are not serving the poison of wrong doctrine; we are serving the life-giving Word of God."

Hickey keeps very busy, hosting three international ministry events annually—such as the International Women's Conventions—traveling to cities throughout the country giving seminars/miracle crusades and writing a monthly column for *Charisma* magazine. She has been ministering on daily 15-minute radio programs for 12 years, and is heard over 185 stations, seven of which are overseas; and for 11 years on weekly half-hour television programs on 20 television stations and two cable networks.

Hickey's Bible study groups first encouraged her to try radio. But one station manager didn't want her program on the air. A confrontation ensued. "I could have given up when he just kept telling me to call back later," Hickey wrote in *Outpouring*. "I think the same was true with television. There are testing times that we all have in which we really have to fight. I don't think we always need green lights—we need the leading of the Holy Spirit."

Being a pastor's wife and former school teacher helped her cope with the challenge of radio. Shortly thereafter, she began her television ministry. "With radio, it seemed as though I almost stumbled into it because of my Bible study groups," she explained. "But God really spoke clearly to me about a television-teaching ministry. It became such a burning desire in my heart." To her, radio is primarily listened to by Christians and "feeds" them, but television is more of an evangelistic "fishing" tool to reach the unsaved with the gospel.

The peripatetic Hickey shows no signs of slowing down. Asked if it may be time to slacken her pace, she replied, "I don't dare sit back and say, 'I see some good things, so this is it.' I see areas in our ministry that are very fruitful, but the world is dying and going to hell by the billions. So how can we stop now?''

Danuta Rylko Soderman. Danuta likes to laugh. And as the ebullient cohost of the "700 Club," she adds a quick smile and infectious gaiety to that daily news magazine. She has cohosted the show with Ben Kinchlow and Dr. M.G. (Pat) Robertson since March 1983. Robertson, founder and president of the Virginia Beach-based Christian Broadcasting Network (CBN), has been the guiding force behind his professional, glossy TV show since its inception in 1967. (Robertson pioneered the first religious TV station, the first religious network and the first Christian programming to use a talk-show format.) In the United States the "700 Club" is carried on about 190 broadcast stations and is available to about 26 million households via the CBN Cable Network, one of the nation's largest; it is carried worldwide by the American Forces Radio and Television Services and airs in Canada, most of Central America, Argentina, the Philippines, Panama, the West Indies, Puerto Rico, the Virgin Islands, St. Maarten, Mexico, Taiwan, and in Monte Carlo. On a given day, topics discussed on the "700 Club" range from world debt and the arms race to health/fitness tips and behind-the-scenes interviews with entertainers.

But if things begin to get too serious, Danuta helps lighten the mood. One day she brought her pet sheep Emma to the TV studio, and the nervous animal wet on the director's shoes; during a week-long trip to Texas, Danuta dressed up in cowboy boots and hat and with some difficulty, roped (an underhand toss) and branded (with white paint) a plucky calf—much to the amusement of the leather-tough cowboys helping her and Texan Ben Kinchlow.

While not a preacher or teacher-lecturer in the traditional sense, Danuta shoulders her share of duties on the "700 Club." For many viewers, the show's most captivating segment is when Danuta, Pat and Ben join hands and pray for healing for their television audience. The three, with closed eyes and clasped hands, announce healings taking place in what they call a "word of knowledge"—that someone is being healed of cancer or bursitis or an ear infection, and so on. And after the show, Danuta might fly off to Missouri with a film crew to talk with a jet pilot or to New York to interview the prime minister of Israel; she has interviewed such national figures as Jeane Kirkpatrick, Edwin Meese, Bob Dole and George Bush.

In fact, Danuta's forte is her skill as an interviewer. On the "700 Club" she is allowed to ask questions not often asked, questions about the spiritual and moral dimension of people in public life. And sometimes she directs her inquiries—pulling questions from a large, yellow bag—to Pat Robertson. It is openly acknowledged that Robertson's book *Answers to 200 of Life's Most Probing Questions* was based on 20 hours of questions and answers between him and Danuta in a recording studio.

In high school Danuta set her sights on a career in broadcast journalism. She studied communications at the University of Colorado, then left a masters program in philosophy and journalism at Colorado to become the first female camera operator in Phoenix; after two years she went to San Francisco and was hired by a news service to give radio ski reports. After the ski season, Danuta was offered work as a radio news reporter in San Diego, and soon became the cohost of "Sun-Up San Diego," a morning television talk show. During her five years there she entertained audiences with the same flair and excitement that have made her popular with "700 Club" viewers. But Danuta was on a spiritual search as well: studying tarot cards, Zen Buddhism, macrobiotics, transcendental meditation, the *I Ching* and dabbling in an esoteric Eastern religion called the Nairishirin Daishonen. And she became involved in a philosophy discussion group, which later became a Bible study group that was responsible for her eventual conversion to conservative Christianity.

In March 1983 Danuta was invited by CBN for an audition; two weeks later she packed up and left the California palms for Virginia Beach, Virginia. She is now married to Kai Soderman, a financial consultant.

Danuta once told a reporter she was annoyed because there weren't more strong female personalities in the church: "It's O.K. to have opinions, to be assertive, to be strong." She wants people to enjoy life more. "I see a lot of people walking around with hunched backs and lowered eyes, afraid to speak, afraid to laugh, afraid to enjoy the life God has given them," she says. Having always been active in the outdoors—teaching swimming, sky diving, white-water rafting, racing sports cars and scuba diving—Danuta wants to climb Mount Kilimanjaro with her husband. As *The Saturday Evening Post* described her, "Traditional she is not. A lively role model she is."

Anne Giminez. Upon This Rock is a barebones biography that tells the story of how an ex-heroin addict from the Bronx, John Giminez, met and eventually married Pentecostal evangelist Anne E. Nethery from Corpus Christi, Texas. The two slowly fashioned a ministry that is becoming a rising star. Before their marriage, Anne had spent most of her life working in the church and realized she was taking a sizable risk with John; many people had told her to get away from him "before you're tainted too." And she had to contend with her own parents' bigotry: John was Puerto Rican and the Netherys associated his Hispanic features as being Mexican; in their Texas town, Mexicans were at the bottom of the social ladder.

But the wedding went ahead as planned in September 1967. The shaky husband-and-wife ministry had to overcome a number of obstacles on the road to Rock Church in Virginia Beach, Virginia. One nagging problem was tight finances, another was covert and overt prejudice against women preachers. Yet the Giminezes persevered, even appearing on the "700 Club"—John gave his testimony and he and Sister Anne sang scripture choruses. While looking in the area for a church of their own, they stayed with Jim and Tammy Bakker, who worked with CBN at the time. The Giminezes finally became the pastors of Rock Church (John: "God said we're going to build on the solid rock. The rock that is Jesus Christ."), a rented, white frame building in Norfolk, Virginia.

CBN was an important booster for them in those days. The Gimenezes appeared a few more times on the "700 Club." John's past experience in the drug culture and ministry to addicts impressed local businessmen, who helped him gain appearances before civic groups and high school assemblies. John's counseling efforts became so successful they caused friction between him and Anne; she felt he was focusing too much on youth work to the detriment of pastoring their church. After a "divine intervention" and the birth of a baby girl, the conflict was suitably resolved.

A series of articles on the Jesus Movement captured the pages of *Life* magazine and the country's interest in the late 1960s and early 1970s. Rock Church became flooded with young people; crowds grew so large the building was becoming a fire hazard. A new Rock Church was later built on five and a half acres on Kempsville Road, and was dedicated in May 1971. Said Anne, "Just as the Lord had promised—when the doors were opened—everything was paid for." Crowds jammed the new structure, and a balcony and adjoining education building were added.

But some area residents and several local ministers were bothered by Anne's ministry; the struggle over her right to preach caused a great deal of stress and even fallings-out with friends and colleagues. One radio preacher began referring to a mysterious woman preacher he called "the witch of Kempsville." Sister Anne had no doubt whom the man was speaking about.

Within two years, Rock Church had outgrown its available space. It was time to build again. This time the new sanctuary would be round— seating 3,000—with a platform area housing a 100-voice choir and orchestra. Men from the church helped in the construction and donated thousands of dollars worth of electrical supplies and services. Dedication came in May 1977.

Next, the Giminezes hit the airwaves. With the help of CBN's broadcasting professionals, "Rock Church Alive!" aired in May 1978. The program consists of worship services held in Rock Church and, as John describes, "shows the joy and worship in our services." But along with success, a price was being paid. The Gimenez schedule was pressure-packed with counseling appointments and various meetings; the phone rang constantly, and during one month, they did three programs a week instead of one. Sister Anne nearly had a nervous breakdown. But healing came gradually during an extended vacation. "When I look back now at the situation," she said, "I can see the devil was trying to destroy me. It was such an ordeal."

Now their ministry has a Bible Institute, Rock Christian Academy, affiliate churches, a children's home in India and church-supported missionaries. Sister Anne's new book, *The Emerging Christian Woman*, was published. Once, during a public hearing over the church's girls' home, (the City of Kempsville had ordered it closed) a frustrated woman asked, "You people promised us you'd just be a neighborhood church when you moved here. You're not a neighborhood church...in fact you're not a national church. You're a *worldwide* church. But what I want to know is when is Rock Church gonna quit growing?"

The room was quiet for a moment. Then a lone voice from another corner of the room suggested, "Why Don't you ask God, lady?"

Beverly LaHaye. Mrs. LaHaye is a Christian moralist-activist and head of Concerned Women for America (CWA). While she is not very well known in the secular media, in 1985 she was chosen by a national conservative magazine as being the fifth most admired conservative woman in America—right behind Jeane Kirkpatrick and Nancy Reagan. In Christian circles her name has clout; she and her husband, Pastor Tim LaHaye, conducted 465 family-life seminars in 42 countries; she was the cohost of a weekly TV show and call-in radio talk show. Pastor Tim told of the time they were on the way to a Dallas "March Against Porn" rally and Beverly slipped while running to catch a plane. A bone in her foot was broken, but she refused to have the foot set in a cast because she would have missed the rally. So they bought some crutches and she hobbled up to the platform.

"She is one tough lady!" the LaHayes' doctor reportedly exclaimed. But she hasn't always been "tough" says Pastor Tim. God has helped her there, and the humanists and feminists have forced it upon her.

LaHaye often tells the story about how CWA got started. She was listening to Betty Friedan, founder of the National Organization for Women, tell Barbara Walters about *The Feminine Mystique*. Friedan not only gave the strong impression during the conversation that she was representing the women of America, but that she planned to devote considerable energy to making America a humanist nation. Not "humanitarian" or "human rights," but humanist: a word that describes a person who espouses the philosophy of secular humanism—one of the most poisonous and diabolical of enemies, according to conservative Christians. Little did Friedan realize that her interview was, at that moment, wakening a dozing giant. Beverly LaHaye was incensed. She later encouraged a small group of women in San Diego to organize meetings to educate others about NOW, ERA and other feminist issues. That was 1979—the giant had opened its eyes.

Now headquartered in Washington, D.C., CWA perceives its mission as shoring up the beleaguered American family, combating moral rot and decay, and organizing prayer networks. Prayer and action! is the rallying cry for Beverly's determined troops—some 540,000 strong (and rising). Her warriors are steadfastly pro-life and anti-child abuse; they favor a voluntary-prayer amendment but oppose the ERA; they deplore laws that grant special protection to homosexuals; and they champion parents' rights to direct the upbringing of their children in educational and religious matters. CWA members include all ethnic groups and ages (and some men), from energetic grandmotherly types to crisply suited dress-for-successors. CWA currently boasts active chapters in all 50 states. At one San Diego area meeting, held in the chapel of a local church, a table at the back of the room contained pro-life pamphlets and fact sheet packets. Some of the material described in detail fetal development, abortion procedures, the psychological effects of abortion (anger, depression, regret, recurrent nightmares, guilt, attempted suicide, among others) and answered the question, When Does Life Begin? Answer: biologically at conception.

These Christian activists keep tabs on, and become engaged in, court cases around the country that they believe affect their religious interests. For example, in one case in Florida, two Christian girls (ages 9 and 14) were being persecuted because of their desire to include Christ in Christmas. One girl wanted to pass out stickers with a picture of Jesus as Christmas gifts to classmates—the teacher stopped her. The other drew a nativity scene for a school art contest, but was ordered to destroy it. In a Tel-a-gram to her women, LaHaye wrote: "Case Urgently important. If we win, any school district in America which decides to censor historical truth of Christ's birth will face civil rights action for their illegal actions." CWA is involved in such litigation around the country, and the women warriors often bump up against either the ACLU or Norman Lear and his People for the American Way. LaHaye thinks Lear and his organization are anti-family and anti-God. And she claims that Lear has some well-heeled attorneys from Harvard and Washington, D.C. at the ready to fight some of the more important cases for People for the American Way. (The implication being that the relatively money-poor CWA is being "outgunned" by the high-priced legal help bought by secular humanist megabucks.)

At a lectern, LaHaye is not a dominating presence; one simply sees a middle-aged woman of average appearance and normal build and height; a pastor's wife and mother of four, sometimes neatly decked out in a powder-blue suit with matching blue neckerchief and eye shadow. A CWA pin gleams on her coat lapel. Her fluffed blonde hair forms a bubble-like coiffure above pencil-thin eyebrows. *Mystique*, relates Beverly, gave a scathing report on family life, it denounced men and "ripped marriage apart and left you just stripped of any hope that marriage could ever work." That philosophy began to be reflected in the media and taught in the colleges. Friedan went on to become one of the signers of the Humanist Manifesto, and earn a Humanist of the Year Award. LaHaye believes that humanism comes from humankind's atheistic and egotistic desires. And since its thrust is to rid society of anything that is God-like or God-inspired, we see our increasingly Godless society throwing prayer out of schools.

"Where were we?" LaHaye asks her women. "If we had been organized like we are today, we could have had the network of prayer and action groups, I don't think that could ever have been accomplished.... And humanism began to build and grow. And who are they after? They're after our young people." So the battle for young minds rages. LaHaye often recites Gloria Steinem's now-famous proclamation that by 2,000 A.D. children will have been trained to believe in Man's potential, not God's.

"Pornography is on the rampage in America," LaHaye says. And she adamantly supports the actions taken against "the satanic, filthy lyrics in some rock music." We've had an alarming flare-up of teenage suicide today, she points out. Rock music teaches a low value of human life and that suicide is a way out when things aren't going right. Another of CWA's foes is Planned Parenthood. One book, *Changing Bodies, Changing Lives*, recommended by Planned Parenthood, will not make CWA's recommended-reading list. One section that especially caught

LaHaye's eye was a chapter about exploring sex with someone else. She especially disliked its message that sex with a friend is positive and good, and a description of how to perform oral sex to prevent pregnancy.

But LaHaye remains upbeat: "As I travel around this country, I see more and more people waking up...willing to roll up their sleeves and do something about it.... I think God is going to use us to turn the tide from becoming a humanist nation."

Rexella Van Impe. In the introduction to its television programs, the Van Impe ministry uses rapidly moving images, somewhat like a kaleidoscope, that give viewers a visual impression of an energetic, dynamic organization. With London's Big Ben flashing by on the left side of the screen and a Holy Land scene whizzing past on the right, one gets the impression of a worldwide ministry engaged in important works. And from center-screen, Dr. Jack Van Impe and his wife, Rexella, smile out at their television audience.

The Van Impe organization is based in Royal Oak, Michigan. A ministry profile sheet says Jack Van Impe is an authority on Bible prophecy and is known as "the walking Bible." He claims to have memorized more than 10,000 Bible verses. Wife Rexella is a classical pianist and is often called the "First Lady of Sacred Music" by the gospel music industry. The photogenic, middle-aged husband-and-wife team makes a most attractive couple.

The Van Impes' hour-long television specials borrow some of the eye-catching methods used by professionals in secular television. For example, during one program Rexella was singing in an outdoor amphitheater. While she sang, the camera kept slowly panning around her in a complete circle—a rather glitzy, showbiz technique one would expect in a Barbra Streisand video.

Jack Van Impe met his future wife during one of his evangelistic crusades, and they married in 1952. They crisscrossed the country, holding over a thousand meetings and crusades. Van Impe began a weekly nationwide radio program in 1972, then began a weekly half-hour program in 1980. In 1985 the Van Impes stopped their television programs to produce several hour-long television specials on topics such as the occult andArmageddon; during those programs Rexella usually sings a few songs and conducts an interview with guests. Husband Jack delivers the message/sermon.

The Van Impes hope to launch an ambitious seven-year plan to evangelize the entire nation and Canada—via 15 to 20 citywide crusades a year. Their goal is to win a *million* souls for the Lord. And an upcoming television special on "the great AIDS cover-up" is in the works. They are also preparing to return to a weekly television program. The couple has called for "a new beginning" in which their ministry rededicates itself to being led by the power of the Holy Spirit.

Elizabeth Clare Prophet. One of the very few New Ager's on television, Prophet is much less well known than Terry Cole-Whittaker was in the latter's heyday. But Prophet, known as "Guru Ma" or "Mother of the Flame" to her disciples (a.k.a. "chelas"), has a much more eclectic theology and controversial past than her New Age sister.

Quite simply, the 45-year-old Prophet rules a multi-million dollar religious organization, headquartered on a 260-acre estate near Malibu, California, along with her fourth husband, Edward Francis. The estate is called "Camelot." According to the *Los Angeles Herald*, her Church Universal and Triumphant (CUT) owns a publishing house, a gold mine, several mansions and 3,000 acres of Montana ranch land. Prophet claims to be the reincarnation of Queen Guinevere and Marie Antoinette, among others, and that she is a medium of truth endorsed by the Ascended Masters (beings who have passed on to an elevated spirit plane). Those who follow her teachings, as received from the Great White Brotherhood (a community of Ascended Masters said to be sages of hidden wisdom and knowledge), will have their souls purified by the Violet Consuming Flame so that they may achieve Christ-consciousness.

If all that leaves you rather befuddled, you're in good company. One has to be grounded in New Age religious thought and metaphysics to grasp even the first level of CUT's theology.

Much of that theology is based upon "The Mighty I AM" cult, the creation of Guy and Edna Ballard, occultists and Theosophists in the early twentieth century. The Ascended Masters make up a body of super saints from all races and religious backgrounds who have "ascended" the cycle of birth and rebirth and are now fully "God realized" souls; they dwell in a spiritual dimension and communicate with us through their appointed "Messenger"—Prophet is regarded as the only official "messenger" on the earth today. Foremost among the Ascended Masters is Saint Germain, a French eighteenth-century occultist. His associates in this spirit realm include Jesus the Christ, Master Kuthumi, Master Godfre, Lady Leto, El Morya, Ray-O-Light and others—a pantheon that prompted one magazine writer to remark that it "reads like roll call at Marvel Comics."

Building on the spiritualistic concepts of the Ballards and other Theosophists, Mark L. Prophet founded CUT (known then as Summit Lighthouse) in 1958. He met Elizabeth (nee Wulf) in Boston in 1961 and they were married two years later. Mark, twenty years her senior, died of a stroke in 1973, and is now deemed to be an Ascended Master. The teachings, as preached by the latter and mediumistically dictated through Guru Ma to her chelas, posit that each person is believed to be on a spiritual pilgrimage (through many reincarnations) from the lower self to the higher self. Among the practices aimed at helping in this pilgrimage is the use of "decrees," a high-speed chanting of incantations; a favorite is, "I am that I am," an affirmation of self-deity that ensures ascension. Devotees also seek to cleanse their karma by being surrounded by the "Violet Consuming Flame," a sacred fire said to be made available by the spiritual merit of St. Germain.

CUT's television programs are aired primarily in California, but can also be seen in Alaska, Arizona, Colorado and Connecticut. The organization sends videotapes to local groups, which, in turn, submit them for viewing on public access (cable) television stations. As a personal observation, I find Prophet to be a competent, articulate preacher, but her performance is marred by too few gestures, not enough body movement and a speaking voice that often lapses into a droning monotone.

CUT's theology would seem to appeal to individuals interested in Eastern religions with a Christian frame of reference; some are attracted by the awe of receiving directly from Prophet's lips what they believe are supernatural messages of departed spiritual masters. CUT is also outspokenly patriotic and politically conservative. Guru Ma believes the citizens of America are a chosen people who are destined to save the planet from communism. "Our 50 states are the reincarnation of the 12 tribes of Israel," she has told her 150,000 followers. "This is the New Jerusalem. This is the Promised Land."

Quo Vadis?

Still other women could be cited: Gloria Copeland—the strong right arm of the Kenneth Copeland Ministries—has often preached on television, at conventions/crusades and specializes in healing; and Jan Crouch plays a strong "side-kick" role in her husband's ministry. This is not new, however. According to William C. Martin (chairperson of the Sociology Department at Rice University), back in Billy Sunday's day his wife was really the brains behind the business side of their organization.

For years it was the fashion for some women "side-kicks" to write appeal letters or notes aimed mostly toward the women in the television audience. But gradually, explained Martin, more evangelists brought their wives into the foreground. "It probably is as much a function of their just saying, 'Well, let's go along with this and let's see if it works. You can do it, babe.' They did it and it worked all right." The more prominent role of women in the electric church most likely reflects the movement

Gloria and Kenneth Copeland

of women into more and more leadership positions throughout society. Certain churches, too, have proven more amenable to such advances. From the beginning, Pentecostal and charismatic churches have allowed women the freedom to become spiritual leaders.

While the electric sisters have been emerging onto the ecclesiastical stage from the wings and virtually all denominations are moving toward female ordination, this progression by no means represents a groundswell. But the phenomenon *is* occurring, and the churches will—as they nearly always do—reflect the larger society.

****

Modern communications technology is powerful. Our consciousness is influenced and shaped by the messages we receive through mass communications. According to sociologist Jeffrey Hadden, the great contest now taking place is the struggle for access to, and control of, that technology. Both political and religious conservatives have the upper hand in the use of this technology, and today we are witnessing an ideological battle of sorts; this battle has a lot to do with what our government does in our lives.

There is an active countermobilization of people and organizations that oppose what has been called the New Christian Right. Hadden believes the leaders of the electric churches are only now beginning to be influential. "The outcome," he writes in *Prime Time Preachers*, "will determine the direction of American society as we move into the twenty-first century." And while the women preachers and moralists may not be as visible, mediawise, as the Jimmy Swaggarts or Jerry Falwells, they will be playing out their own unique roles in this human drama. And support or advocacy for causes/issues need not have a high profile to be effective. In fact, Hadden points out that it is not of any great significance that most of the electric church preachers are not now in politics. In their search to broaden their ministries, both male and female preachers will be adding to the foundation of a potentially powerful social movement—the resurgence of conservative influence—that aspires to return our nation to God.

The 1960's had its "death of God" controversy and the late 1960's saw the penetration of American culture by Eastern religions. Since then we have experienced a proliferation of "new religious expressions." Yet in all of this religious ferment, some experts believe that the growth of evangelistic faiths has been the largest, and the latter has had the greatest immediate influence on our culture. So this is the struggle to reshape America, and it will happen, in part, on our television screens. Television not only mirrors our values, it helps shape them as well.

And how the electric preachers use their enormous power base will have important implications for this country's future.

Contemporary Christian Music: Rock The Flock

Bill Young

In the late 1960s contemporary Christian music consisted of a handful of performers playing wherever and whenever they could. They survived on their word-of-mouth reputations, independently pressed albums, and cheaply reprinted flyers heralding performances in private homes, small halls, and occasionally a progressive church auditorium.

Today Gospel music has much more in common with Bruce Springsteen than George Beverly Shea and the new message from Christian musicians is "Let it Rock" according to Billboard magazine. Quoting secular recording artist Greg Kihn, "Contemporary Christian music is a major force now. It's an actual musical genre." No doubt that one of the reasons that contemporary Christian music is broadening is that it is becoming more and more commercial. Jon Anderson, founder of YES had this to say "To me contemporary Christian music is the station that I tune in on the radio, thinking that I'm hearing secular music because it sounds so hip, until I catch the words and realize the lyrics have a slightly different intent."

My own feelings about contemporary Christian music is that it's getting better all the time. And its message is put into a format that appeals so much to the listener. It s chief audience is the generation of the New Squares, primarily young whites, 24 to 35, who like the beat of rock but disavow the drugs and sexual permissiveness that are associated with it. I might be a New Square, but I'll never forget the day I was riding down the road and in searching the dial heard this incredible music—one song right after another. I wasn't really zeroing in on the lyrics but after about four songs I realized it was contemporary Christian music. And WRFD of Columbus, Ohio became and still is my station of choice to hear powerhouse rock and roll—Christian style. A style of music that is the music of the 80's.

Indistinguishable—except for their lyrics—from their secular counter-parts, Christian rockers represent one of the most interesting, fast-growing trends in the music world: Christian contemporary music, or evangelical pop. Approximately 15 million contemporary Christian albums were sold in 1984, which helped gospel become the fifth-largest selling category of music—bigger than classical or jazz. To understand its growth one has to go back to the roots of the Jesus movement of the late 60's, for the rise of Jesus music reflects an amazing turnabout in public taste.

When the Jesus movement hit North America in the late 1960s and early 70's, a great many young people converted to the Christian faith and a lot of new music was written in the idiom of the youth culture. The lyrics were genuine and fresh and dealt with the needs of the vast number of New Christians.

Disc jockey Paul Baker, who had begun to collect examples of the new Jesus music, aired the first "all-Jesus rock radio show" on station WLCY in St. Petersburg, Florida. Said Baker, "In the true spirit of a rock and roll disc jockey, I wanted to shock everyone. Not in a negative way, but in a way which would open everyone's eyes to the reality that there could be dynamic rock music about the Maker." But Christian recording labels and Christian bookstores were very resistant to the new evangelical rock, as good old-fashioned southern gospel music still prevailed in the eyes of their audiences—churchgoers.

In fact the two albums which are believed to be the beginnings of Christian contemporary music were released on secular labels. The first, 1969's "Upon This Rock" was created by Larry Norman, the pop music dropout who became the poet laureate of the Jesus revolution. He expressed the exuberant spirit of the movement with "Wowie, Zowie, He Saved My Soul!" and later released the evangelical rock anthem "Why Should the Devil Have all the Good Music?" The second important release was 1970's "Mylon" by Mylon LeFevre, the songwriter and session man who was once kicked out of Bob Jones University for singing Jesus jazz. His album was one of the first gospel rock albums released on Cotillion records, a secular label which successfully introduced many southern rock groups to the world. LeFevre, who was the founder of the Atlanta Rhythm Section, performed briefly with the dope-indulging Holy Smoke Doo Dah Band, as well as with such notables as George Harrison, Willie Nelson, and the Who. In 1978 LeFevre kicked a drug habit and became a full-fledged Christian rock singer, who with his band Broken Heart, count their success in converts rather than in cash.

After the release of these two landmark albums, the Jesus movement really took off. In June 1971, Jesus graced the cover of Time magazine, and the accompanying story concluded that "Jesus is alive and well in the radical spiritual fervor of a growing number of young Americans who have proclaimed an extraordinary religious revolution in his name." About this same time in Fort Wayne, Indiana, a young Christian named Bob Hartman planted the roots of what was to become the premier Christian rock band of the 1980s—Petra, which means rock in Greek. Hartman, a student at the Christian Training Academy who happened to play guitar (and the only original member still with Petra), joined with John DeGroff on bass, Bill Glover on drums, and Greg Hough on guitar to form Petra.

The Jesus movement was in full swing allowing Petra to be more easily accepted than they would have been either a few years earlier or later. Performances by Petra in the early 70's were generally in high school assemblies, at colleges, or in open parks. Because of great popularity in the Hoosier state, the band traveled to Nashville in 1973 in hopes of landing a recording contract. Late in 1973 the band signed with Myrrh records, a company that was pioneering what was a new and unknown market, that of "Jesus-rock" music. In 1974, the debut album appeared, recorded for a mere $900 in two weeks. Self titled, Petra was not a pacesetting album in terms of sales. Christian stores were not particularly receptive to the new Jesus music and were skeptical at best of anyone who would create such an album. In spite of slow sales, Petra was generating a reputation for rousing live performances and in 1976 they went into the studio to record their second album for Myrrh, "Come and Join Us." This was a very important time in the history of Petra as Bob Hartman invited Greg X. Volz to be guest vocalist. Volz had been lead vocalist for the "e" band, a Jesus rock group out of St. Louis, and to understand the caliber of his singing, it helps to know that he turned down an offer to be lead singer for REO Speedwagon.

When it was released, "Come and Join Us," was also a slow seller. The music was louder and even more powerful, making it less interesting to Christian store managers at the time. Sales were very poor and Petra's recording days with Myrrh were finished. But the band pressed on. Live performances were the only source of income, and they continued honing their craft all over the country. While touring without a record contract, a young visionary record label, Starsong Records, approached the band with an offer. This time Petra went into a different studio complex, with another producer, and their sound began to change from pure rock to pop rock. And the new album "Washes Whiter Than," yielded the band's first radio hit, "Why Should the Father Bother?" The substantial airplay received by the song made Petra known in places where they had never been heard of before. But in 1980 Petra received the breakthrough that they had been praying for.

Jonathan David Brown was brought in to be the producer of the groups fourth album, "Never Say Die." As the recording of "Never Say Die" progressed, Petra remembered the importance of radio airplay in creating demand for their previous LP, so "The Coloring Song" was recorded with that in mind, and the single quickly rose to the top of the contemporary Christian charts. Flushed by their success, the group took to the road and in 1982 performed 161 concerts. They took five weeks off in June of 1982 to record "More Power to Ya." which yielded three major radio hits, "Stand Up," "Road to Zion," and "Let Everything That Hath Breath." The Band then went on to perform 152 more concerts the next year and then in August of 1983 recorded what went on to become the biggest-selling Christian record of all-time "Not of This World." This was the third Petra album produced by Jonathan David Brown, who has molded the band's sound as we know it today.

In the summer of 1984 Petra toured Europe for the first time. The band headlined the annual Christian music and arts festival in Greenbelt, England. And in November of 1984 they released their current album "Beat the System" in which Petra continues to perfect the arena-rock sound that made it the top rock group in religious music. And while "Beat the System" is less a progression than a perfection of that hard rock sound, Petra always gives the people what they want.

"Our band is not in competition with other Christian bands" states Hartman. "We feel we are competing with Journey, Styx, and REO Speedwagon. We need to be aware of them, because the people who come to see Petra go to see those bands as well. We are being naive if we don't keep that in mind. We need to have a light system, sound system, and presentation that will be competitive with those groups."

Soon there may be a day when Petra meets its competition and plays to vast multitudes in the big arenas. But the band has long ago surpassed its competition with the greatest purpose of all: to minister the gospel.

Recently though, the Lord has presented the group with another challenge as vocalist Volz has left the group. Stepping into his spot will be John Schlitt, formerly of the secular rock quintet *Head East*. Meanwhile a double-album live set of the "Beat the system Tour," and a concert video are the groups current projects.

At the same time Bob Hartman was studying at the Christian Training Academy in 1972, the roots of two other major contemporary Christian rock bands were being formed. After accepting Christ, Glenn and Wendy Kaiser formed a now well-known Christian rock community on the north side of Chicago—Jesus People U.S.A. They formed a band as an evangelical tool alongside Glenn's preaching and Wendy's journalistic abilities. The Resurrection Band, often known simply as the Rez Band, bills their sound as "Music to Raise the Dead." Their first album "Awaiting your reply" was critically acclaimed as the first successful heavy-metal Christian music release. In his review in the Illinois Entertainer, Wayne Jancille stated "It's near perfect high energy rock. The talent is there and the feeling. Quite possibly its even because of the band's religious beliefs that this album succeeds. Whatever the case there's so much pleasing rock and roll noise on this record that its hard not to see how agnostics and atheists alike could not help but get off on possibly rock and roll's first true integration with religion."

The band has gone on to be one of Christian rocks most popular live acts, witness their biggest-selling album "Live Bootleg" which features some of their most popular songs such as "Military Man," "City Streets," and "Can't Stop Lovin You."

Songs tackling chemical and physical abuse, war, racism, hypocrisy, repression, and related evils have become their trademark, delivered with the uncompromising one-two punch of Rez Band's singular rock 'n' roll. In its decade-plus of existence, Rez Band has garnered numerous critical plaudits from both trade and consumer press alike. "On the one hand, it should be compared to the cream of the iron crop, like Motley Crue or Scorpions"; wrote Dan Wittle in the Illinois Entertainer "Yet because of its content, Rez Band music exists on another plane entirely."

And that language has multiplied over the years as a result of many new entertainers that are creating sounds that have never been heard in churches. The election of Jimmy Carter, a born-again Christian, gave Jesus music a big boost and the ascent of Ronald Regan propelled it into the big-time. Southern California, always the first with the new, is the biggest market for evangelical rock. And coming out of Cypress, California, is the relentless heavy-metal band Stryper, whose name is inspired by Isaiah 53.5 "with His stripes we are healed." They are perhaps best known for 1984's Heaven and Hell tour, when they opened for the secular band Motley Crue. But instead of throwing drumsticks into the audience, Stryper tosses out about 500 imitation-leather copies of the New Testament. "We are rock and roll evangelists" says drummer Robert Sweet, "Stryper is a modern-day John the Baptist crying in the world

Rez

of rock for those who don't have the life of Christ to turn on the light switch. Our message is J-E-S-U-S."

Shane Hayden, a 17 year-old senior at Wilson High School in Hacienda Heights, California saw Stryper for the first time in 1984 at the LaMiranda Civic Center near Los Angeles. Though he came dreading "choirbells" or the like, he left with a "spiritual high" and says he's been "straight ever since." Part of it was the music. "I've seen Motley Crue, I saw Styx, Kiss, Triumph, Iron Maiden. To me Stryper blows 'em away."

Stryper is only one of dozens of groups preaching the same timeless message in new ways. But perhaps the biggest trend is that of Reborn Rockers, who've seen the light in usually mid-to-late career. And the call to Christianity means a radical change of scenery for them.

In 1983, Kansas, the hugely successful band, where Kerry Livgren built a reputation as one of the great composers in the school of classically influenced rock, underwent some drastic changes. And in 1984, Livgren and bassist Dave Hope formed their own Christian group, A.D., with visions of playing Christian music in the secular marketplace. Their first album, Time Line, was a disappointment as CBS records gave it no promotion what-so-ever. Livgren was quoted as saying "In terms of a ministry what we're doing is very gratifying and fulfilling. In a business sense, though, we're operating in the red. The Christian music business has been somewhat of a disappointment."

But 1985 marked a change of fortune for A.D. as "Art of the State" released by Kerygma Records has proven to be a hit with both radio programmers and the Christian rock community. Livgren notes that "Art of the State" is a "concerted effort not to sound like Kansas." And recent live performances are showing that the band has become stronger and a more defined unit on stage. It's unavoidable for the comparison to Kansas to be brought up, but unlike the last few years of Kansas, A.D. is playing like a band and their enjoyment seem contagious.

The contagious burst of spiritual fervor of the early 70's brought one master musician early into the Christian rock fold. Phil Keaggy was the lead guitarist and vocalist for Glass Harp, a northeastern Ohio band that in the early seventies opened for such diverse acts as the Who, Grand Funk, and Eric Clapton. The Glass harp made three albums during the early 70's including the critically acclaimed "Synergy," and Keaggy's songwriting abilities and performing style lead to many comparisons to Paul McCartney. When Keaggy accepted the Lord in 1973 and decided to devote his talents to Christian rock, rumors that Jimi Hendrix was an ardent admirer of Keaggy and the fact that he'd played with everyone

in the business, lead to immediate acceptance in the Christian music field. Like the "Paul is dead" rumors that started controversy for the Beatles, the question of whether Jimi Hendrix actually stated that Phil Keaggy is the world's greatest guitarist on a nationwide television show, has never been settled. But there's been no question about Keaggy's prowess as a Christian rock artist. In 1980 he released the first all-instrumental Christian rock album, "the Master and the Musician." In 1983 he recorded his biggest selling album, "Play Thru Me," which contained the radio hits, "Happy," "The Wall," and "Play Thru Me." In 1982 the single "Wished You Were There" from Keaggy's "Town to Town" album was the first single on a Christian record label to be released into the non-gospel market. Keaggy said this about his involvement in contemporary Christian music, "Jesus rock was a spontaneous product of the Jesus movement of the early 70's. I came out of that movement using the music I knew best—rock."

In 1975 another noted musician was led to the cross by a fellow band member. Richie Furay became a Christian when he was part of the Southern-Hillman-Furay Band, after becoming involved in a Bible study with guitarist Al Perkins. While still in the S-H-F Band, Furay penned an article for Crawdaddy magazine entitled "A Good Feeling to Know." It was a classic statement of early, bold Christian testimony in the secular music press. A two-page statement of faith, complete with scripture references.

Once the critics and reviewers knew he was "one of those Christians," they began to destroy any of his artistic contributions to the band. Furay left to become a Christian recording artist and released the classic "I've Got a Reason," a stunning hybrid collection of Christian and secular music. The problem was that Atlantic records had no idea of how to promote the album. They suggest to Furay that he should come up with a band, probably remember-membering his success as a founding member of the Buffalo Springfield, Poco, and the S-H-F band.

In 1980 Furay formed USR—United States Rock, a group made up entirely of Christians. Included were noted guitarist Hadley Hockensmith on lead and ex-Poco cohort George Grantham on drums. Atlantic viewed the band as their replacement for Firefall which had left the label. Furay wanted to do nothing but Christian material, and when Atlantic wouldn't budge from their secular aims, Furay disbanded USR, without a single demo tape being made, and continued his solo career.

Al Perkins who had led Furay to the savior, got together with fellow Christians, Chris Hillman, of the Byrds, Flying Burrito Brothers, Manassas, Fame, and Bernie Leadon, ex of the Eagles to form their own contemporary Christian group. Traveling around the country in a van, doing the hard road miles, these professionals are now seeing a much different standard of achievement than what they've been used to. Although one might see their move as one from the major league of secular rock to the bush league of contemporary Christian music, many other rockers have made themselves accountable to God instead of the dollar sign.

Other noted Jesus rock artists include Dan Peek, formerly of America, Michael Omartian of Loggins and Messina, Rick Cua of the Outlaws, Joe English of Paul McCartney and Wings, Leon Patillo of Santana, and Graham Goble and Been Birtles of Australia's Little River Band.

Certainly one of the fast-growing areas of Christian rock is Heavy Metal. Besides the aforementioned Stryper, heavyweights included Europe's top Christian band, Jerusalem, Saint, The Messiah Prophet Band, The Daniel Band, and the Darrell Mansfield Band, featuring ex-members of Cactus and Iron Butterfly. Another popular artist is Reggie Vinson, who co-wrote "Billion Dollar Babies" with Alice Cooper and did vocals and played guitar on Cooper's "School's Out" album.

As contemporary Christian music has branched out, singer/songwriter Steve Taylor has emerged as one of gospel's most popular artists by setting witty, satirical lyrics to fast-paced new-wave beats. Backed by some of Christian rock's finest musicians, Taylor comes off like a gospel Elvis Costello, lambasting politicians, preachers, and others who are out for fame and fortune. Taylor has garnered considerable secular media attention including articles and reviews by publications like the *Los Angeles Times, Houston Post,* and the *Rocky Mountain News.* His songs have also cut inroads in an area still new to Christian music-college radio.

Indeed, Taylor's danceable, highly original syntho-strong compositions have taken the Christian pop genre to heights of innovation previously unscaled. Yet, even more unprecedented, it is by way of his biting, unwhite-washed lyrical perceptions on controversial subject matter—while playing down the stereotypical crusader tendencies—that he harbors the potential to crack the secular barriers wide open. His skillfully-written songs about relevant topics like racism among Christians ("We Don't Need No Colour Code") and religious persecution in Poland ("Over My Dead Body") indicate Taylor's desire to present faith in a realistic way. Whether it is pastors ("I Manipulate") or churches ("This Disco Used to be a Cute Cathedral") Taylor has managed to corner the market on making convicting songs fun and even danceable.

STEVE TAYLOR

One of the popular current Christian artists is Dion, who has become the spokesman for the Catholic Charismatic Movement with his music. Dion claims "that nothing in my past matters at all. The only important thing I've ever done is to bring my mother and sister to Christ." Other former pop stars who now sing only for Christ include Paul Stookey, Barry McGuire, and Anthony Gourdine, the Little Anthony of the Imperials. One of the more interesting bands popular today is David and the Giants, featuring drummer Keith Thibodeaux, the former child actor who portrayed Little Ricky on "I Love Lucy."

Ironically, it was often the converts from secular success who conquered ambivalence and created the most original religious music. The fall of 1979 was a triumph for born-again rock as Bob Dylan, Van Morrison, and Arlo Gutherie issued albums that represented a musical and spiritual rebirth. All three demonstrated for Christians a way in which those who sought the best of both worlds could build rather than burn bridges between the sacred and the secular.

Their attitude continues today in the guise of the band U2. In 1984 for the second year in a row, they took top spot in Contemporary Christian Magazine's Top 10 albums of the year. In his December 1984 review of "The Unforgettable Fire," Quincy Smith-Newcomb explained "While the album doesn't reach the heights of 'war' it marks a necessary stretching point if U2 is to develop into the truly great talent the group's potential indicates, it will be of deep interest to Christians in touch with contemporary artistic endeavors." There's no doubt about the intentions of this band and although all three of U2's studio albums have had a significant amount of spiritual content, its the live "Under a Blood Red Sky" that states their beliefs most clearly and dramatically. Their story is one of Christian artists on an artistic quest. And their quest is important because the mainstream Christians have heard of and know this band.

Less than one percent of all Christians in this country qualify as Christian music enthusiasts. At most five percent of all Christians qualify as moderately aware of Christian music. At least 90 percent of all Christians fall into the mainstream category. So when Rolling Stone magazine declared U2 as their choice for the band of the 80's it was a significant event. The old Jesus tune "Why Should the Devil Have all the Good Music?" becomes relevant as U2 has managed to raise the issues of God and human concern, maintain an uncompromising personal integrity, and command a popular and growing fascination in the rock and roll world. The band has an attitude of being in the world, but not of it.

Today's Christian Rockers seem to be able to handle both the medium and the message. Concerts are entertaining but focused on the Lord. As Petra declares "Our rock is not as their rock," the new Christian rockers are daring to rock the flock. And they are bringing the gospel through the genre of rock to people who have never heard or who have heard, but never thought it could apply to them.

Music videos have become an accepted viable entertainment form and have been responsible for breaking new acts, also helping to build artist recognition and expose new forms of music. One fairly new musical genre, Contemporary Christian Music, has been a little late in getting on the video bandwagon, but has made up for its late start by its video enthusiasm.

Christian videos (are set) apart from secular counterparts by placing evangelism over sales figures. The many Christian performers who have created music videos strongly believe in video as a viable tool for evangelism and ministry, and bringing these Christian rock music videos to public attention is truly a meaningful challenge for the artists. Since MTV is obviously slanted to the secular marketplace, the Christian artists have to prove that Christianity and hard rock can mix. Initially what the genre needed was a breakthrough into rotation on MTV's programming. The artists wanted to reach the rock and roll generation by presenting the gospel with the music that that generation has grown up with. The initial breakthrough was from a band fronted by a duo often referred to as "the Billy Grahams of Contemporary Rock."

Pioneers of carefully crafted Christian rock and roll, DeGarmo and Key recorded the undisputed groundbreaker of Christian rock into MTV, "Six, Six, Six". But it wasn't done without a controversy as the standout cut from the *Communication* album was initially turned down by MTV on the basis of excessive violence, primarily because the video's dream/nightmare vision culminates in an immolation. So the Christian pop duo suddenly found themselves alongside seventy-five secular groups that had videos under review, due to intensive pressure to eliminate heavy violence from the network's videos.

This was not the first obstacle that the band had to try to surpass. When the friends started performing progressive Christian music during the early "70's" no one actually had a name for the type of music the duo was performing. They quickly became labeled as "the Christian Band" and it was a trying time as they were too rock for the Christians and too Christian for the rockers. But the group persevered and their pioneer status did put them on the leading edge of the Contemporary Christian music explosion.

When "Six, Six, Six" was banned by MTV, the group thought that perhaps they were being singled out because they were a Christian group. But this wasn't the case, so the band and it's management agreed to remake the video by removing the offending human torch scene which MTV so strongly objected to. The new scene, shows a man gazing into a crystal ball which features a nuclear holocaust instead of the flaming Antichrist. This was acceptable and MTV programmed the video into rotation and the door was opened to Contemporary Christian music performers.

"Six, Six, Six" was a success and the DeGarmo and Key band followed it up with two other videos which were aired on MTV and other music video shows. These videos "Competition" and "Destined to Win" both feature hard-edged rock with incisive lyrics and the tight vocal harmonies, for which the group is renowned. "Destined to Win" is a strong cut with Dana Key dueting with gospel perennial, Jessy Dixon. "Competition" is a compelling message of a call to repentance for non-Christians.

The newest MTV Christian video stars are the Rez Band, who have been well-known in the Midwest area since their inception in 1972. Their first music video "Crimes", a tale of destitution and redemption has a successful month-long run on MTV. "Crimes" follows a family in which the son is involved with vandalism and drugs, the daughter is a prostitute, and the father a drunk, but in the end they are all redeemed. The video ends with the Rez Band leading a triumphant procession of inner-city dwellers along a Chicago street. Shot in the same neighborhood of uptown Chicago where the band lives, and their spiritual community, Jesus People U.S.A. exists, the video captures the essence of living in the inner-city ghetto and it's woes for families.

The band's latest video "Love Comes Down" also has had an extensive MTV run. Taken from their *Between Heaven 'N Hell* album, its a fun song about God's love coming down and touching an individual's life. Once again, as on "Crimes", Rez stayed within the confines of inner-city Chicago to film at sites such as Von Steuban High School and the Wilson Avenue Elevated train station. The video keeps on the move and the increased budget compared to "Crimes" ($40,000 versus $14,000) shows in the slick production. Undoubtably a move to help bring their music to a wider audience, "Love Comes Down", introduced the Rez Band to a whole new generation of rock music fans.

The two Rez videos have been combined in a commercial package and the video includes interviews with the band and intensive Bible studies. Like DeGarmo and Key's complete video package, "Visions of the Light Brigade", the included Bible studies are intended to be used for personal growth and spiritual challenge, both individually and in group situations.

The video is turning out to be a big seller, most probably because of the fact that the band is musically accomplished. Often referred to as the best heavy-metal group in the Midwest, Christian or Mainstream, the fans are glad to see that the video captures the emotion and talent of the band. The profits of the band are plowed back into the Jesus People U.S.A. Ministry that cares for and feeds up to 300 street people daily, counsels teenage criminals and drug abusers and serves as chaplains for the Cook County Jail. While their music has often been compared to VAN HALEN, AEROSMITH, and AC/DC, it's their sincerity, morality, and conviction that separates them.

Christian Rocks' newest video star is a youth-pastor turned new-wave-singer, Steve Taylor. His first video release, "Meltdown (At Madame Tussauds)", based on the title track from Taylor's *Meltdown* LP, has received airplay on several major cable outlets, including "America Rocks", "Rock World", "ABC Los Angeles", "Good Night L.A." and MTV. Taylor produced, directed, and starred in the video which features his sardonic offbeat approach and trendy synthesizer sound. Perhaps because of the above, Taylor has had more appeal to certain segments of the secular community than other Christian artists.

Son of a Baptist minister, Taylor's combination of humor and new-wave gospel, plus his interest in learning all he could about the state of video art, provided refreshing, watchable videos. His current video products include "The Fritz Movie", a 30 minute long-form video in support of his *On The Fritz* album; "Videoworks", which features his video 45 "Meltdown (At Madame Tussauds)"; "Lifeboat", in which Steve portrays Mrs. Aryan who explains the concept of "values clarification" to her elementary school class; and two excerpts from his forthcoming concert video "Limelight". "Videoworks" also includes interview footage, which like the "Limelight" concert, was filmed at the Greenbelt Music Festival in England, where Taylor was seen as the key show stealer at the festival. The two live tunes, "On the Fritz" and "I Want To Be A Clone", serve tremendous appetizers for the full-length concert video. "Lifeboat" is an effective video and portrays a daring game of perfection (Played over lazy calypso rhythms) by Mrs. Aryan and her class of young students. All in all, this video is just the kind of thing Christian Music needs; a refreshing, new-wave tinged release that can appeal to todays rock music fans.

Another popular Christian Music video that made MTV audiences aware of the genre was Sheila Walsh's "Mystery" which was from her Grammy nominated *War Of Love* album. Besides MTV, "Mystery" received national exposure on WTBS "Night Tracks" and "America's Music" shows. Sheila, who is Great Britains major contribution to gospel rock, offers rock anthems to shake the soul with songs of troubled marriages and the fear of nuclear war. Walsh, who has her own BBC television show, successfully mixes the sacred and the sexy on her songs and videos. With particular reference to live performance video two prominent names in Contemporary Christian Music, Petra and Michael W. Smith, vie for the honor of having the most exciting full-length concert video. Petra's "Captured in Time and Space" is the video rememberance of their critically acclaimed *Beat The System* Tour which captures most of the magic and ministry of the tour. Certainly the premier hard-techno-rock Christian band, Petra includes old favorites with the current cuts and its impressive stage set-up (borrowed from the *Audiovisions* Tour of the group Kansas) to provide a memorable video. Michael W. Smith, former keyboardist for CCM's reigning star, Amy Grant, and his band come off on video tape as though professionals. Amy, in fact, makes a guest appearance showing up for a duet on Smith's classic ballad "Friends". The video shows a performance that was consistently impressive in musical, technical, visual and spiritual levels.

Another live video that hits the mark is "Sheep in Wolves' Clothing" by Mylon LeFevre and Broken Heart. Basically, this is a fine concert video made interesting by the born-again rockers conviction that souls can be saved at live shows. LeFevre and his band have also recorded concept videos of "Stranger to Danger" and "Trains Up In The Sky". As an ordained minister and elder, LeFevre feels that the video, like the rock and roll show, is a ministry, a celebration of Christ.

Certainly the future f Christian Music Video looks bright to many. But what of the many Christians who believe that video is evil and that it is not of God. Actually aren't they being supported by videos such as "Six, Six, Six" in which everything and everyone in the worlds society are portrayed as evil accomplices of the Antichrist. If Christian artists are using videos as a ministry, can marketing and ministry be combined? If Christian artists are concerned about using videos as an art form, can *art* and ministry be combined with the purpose of commercial profit?

One can't deny that "Six, Six, Six", for example, looks any different from all the other videos on MTV. If you take a look at the Contemporary Christian Music industry its easy to see that it is modeled after its secular counter-part. The only difference is the product and the videos show this. Heavy-metal hitters like Rez and Mylon LeFevre videos proclaim God's redeeming love, while secular heavy-metal bands can commit the most horrible crimes on video. Attention-getting has become the key to successful secular videos and Christian acts are forced to explore the world of cinematic techniques also. But the difference again is the product.

Music and video are only reflections of their creators. People interested in watching videos by Rez, Steve Taylor and DeGarmo and Key on MTV are going to be exposed to videos before and after those artists. One can't deny that some of the secular videos are fun to watch as they play with the theme of the song but it is evident that as the medium of music video has grown, the content has become more and more shocking especially in sexual and violent imagery. The content is certainly not governed by what is considered healthy for young viewers but instead by the Nielson ratings.

A recent Nielson survey revealed that MTV has more influence on record buying than radio, concerts or commercial television shows that Christian artists need to get involved in the video revolution. Importantly, they need to be involved in the secular world of MTV, VH-1 and other music video shows. It has been proven that the release of a video increases record sales anywhere between 25 to 40 percent in those areas that have MTV. If Christian artists and Christians in general are concerned about exploitative and abusive videos that demonstrate the cultural bankruptcy of rock music and its manipulation by marketing entrepreneurs, they need to be involved. One often hears of a need for an alternative video channel programming only acceptable Christian videos with the proper religious sentiments. But what if that happened? Certainly the many people that need to hear the gospel communicated in the guise of rock music would never be reached and that is the main goal to the artists.

In "Six, Six, Six", DeGarmo and Key are telling the world to beware of the number 666 for it is the sign of the Antichrist. In Steve Taylor's "Meltdown (at Madame Tussauds)", he uses the melting wax figures in the museum as symbols of temporal life. In the Rez band's "Crimes" a family in trouble is redeemed. These artists all realize that Christian music needs to be taken to a broader market, a broader public.

There is no doubt that MTV, VH-1 and all the national video venues look at Christian rock as a sub-sub-genre and Christian performers are probably responsible for that belief. Praise lyrics repeated over and over are not going to command viewer interest again and again on video. Perhaps the best example is Sandi Patti, the most popular female Christian singer selling even more albums than Amy Grant. Possessing a beautiful, classically trained voice, she entered the video world with two videos that are plainly meant to appeal to believers, mature believers at that.

Glenn Kaiser of the Rez band perhaps says it best. "In many churches on Sunday you'll hear John 3:16 from the pulpit except the people that need to hear John 3:16 aren't there." That is why Christian rock videos are an important form of ministry. If these performers can take their message outside of the more narrow gospel framework, they can reach many more people. If these videos can bring their message to the common guy on the street with everyday situations, problems, and personal doubts, the future looks bright. An artist by the name of Springsteen hit that vein in popular music with his songs and his "Dancing in the Dark" video opening him up to a vast new audience. If Christian performers can tap that same vein, the ventures into video will be worth it. By making sure Christian videos explore the issues of everyday life, it is a sign the Christian Community at all levels is intent on bringing biblical influence to the video arts, rock theology if you will. Hallelujah!!

The Language of Apocalypse: Premillennialists and Nuclear War

Michael Barkun

Millenarian expectation—the anticipation of imminent, total, collective, supernatural, this-worldly salvation[1]—has flared at the margins of Christianity since the late Middle Ages. The contemporary resurgence of Protestant fundamentalism in America is now the vehicle for yet another millenarian wave. However, the apparatus of modern communications—cable television, video recording, and mass market paperbacks—has brought apocalyptic themes from the theological and social margins, where they traditionally flourished, into the main stream of American cultural awareness. Not since the days of the "Second Great Awakening" before the Civil War have so many Americans been so relentlessly exposed to chiliastic arguments and imagery. These arguments generally rest on the theology of "dispensationalism," a position first developed in England in the 1830's.

Dispensationalism held that history was a sequence of periods or "dispensations." As the final period of history draws to a close, three events will take place in preparation for the millennium itself. First, a seven year period of intense tumult and violence—the "Tribulation"—will engulf the world. Second, Christ will return at the end of the Tribulation to mark the beginning of the millennium. Third, at some point in or immediately before the seven-year "Tribulation," saved Christians will be physically removed from the earth and will exist outside it with Christ until his return. This removal, referred to as the "Rapture," elaborates upon an eschatological New Testament passage:

...the dead in Christ shall rise first, then we which are alive and remain shall be caught up together with them in the clouds, to meet the Lord in the air...[2]

Most contemporary dispensationalists believe in a so-called "pre-Tribulational Rapture," in which Christians, having been removed prior to the Tribulation, will not be affected by the seven years of violence.[3]

The Premillennialist View of Nuclear War

The tone of contemporary chiliastic thought has been set by those who have adopted dispensational premillennialism. Of this group the two individuals who have probably reached the widest and most diverse audiences have been Jerry Falwell and Hal Lindsey, the former through television and the organizational activities of the Moral Majority, the latter through mass market paperback books. In addressing nuclear issues, both Falwell and Lindsey have had to manage the tension between their beliefs that on the one hand history will end by divine intervention, and on the other, that nuclear weapons place the capacity for world destruction in the hands of human beings.

Jerry Falwell initially anticipated a major nuclear war connected with the battle of Armageddon, triggered by a Soviet invasion of the Middle East. As he explained in a 1981 interview, "And it is at that time when I believe there will be some nuclear holocaust on this earth, because it says that blood shall flow in the streets up to the bridle of the horses in the Valley of Esdraelon for some 200 miles."[4] He went on to indicate that although the Soviets will be the aggressors, they will suffer a retaliatory nuclear strike which will kill a substantial portion of the Soviet population.

By 1983, however, Falwell had considerably changed his views. In a pamphlet and accompanying cassette tapes, he minimized the danger of nuclear war. A nuclear war will not occur because "God...is in control." "If God were removed from the events of mankind, everyone would have great reason to be gravely concerned about nuclear war. But praise the Lord, He is intimately involved in the affairs of mankind."[5] Since the United States is to Falwell God's instrument for the evangelization of the world, it must be preserved.

Quite apart from the fate of the United States, Falwell insists that the earth must also be preserved essentially intact in order to serve as the stage upon which the events of the Tribulation and the subsequent millennium can be played out.

There should be no fear that the world is going to be destroyed by nuclear war for a long time. God has other plans. The Millennium is 1,000 years in length and will begin after the seven-year Tribulation period. But none of this can begin until believers in the Lord Jesus Christ are raptured. Therefore, the earliest that a worldwide nuclear confrontation could happen is at least 1,007 years away if Jesus would come for His saints today!

Consequently, "...we don't need to go to bed at night wondering if someone's going to push the button and destroy the planet between now and sunrise...." This does not, of course, entirely dispose of the issue of nuclear weapons, for Falwell does not explicitly address the possibility that tactical nuclear weapons might be used, but even if they were, according to his scenario, their use would not produce the process of escalation often predicted by others. So far as the saved are concerned, these considerations are in any case academic, for "...if you are saved, you will never go through one hour, not one moment of the Tribulation...if Jesus came today, every saved person, every saved person, living and dead, would go up instantly to be in the presence of the Lord." Only the unregenerate would suffer whatever disasters lay in store during the Tribulation.[6]

Whatever Falwell's skepticism concerning the use of nuclear weapons during the Tribulation, he assigns a clear place for them later, when at the close of the millennium, the earth will be destroyed in a nuclear holocaust. A nuclear disaster will usher in eternity:

...this heaven and this earth will one day be destroyed, melted with "fervent heat," and I cannot imagine anything but nuclear holocaust that will do that.... I do believe that nuclear power will be the instrument God uses to destroy the present universe and to bring new heavens, new earth, eternity into being.[7]

The ultimate nuclear weapon will, in short, be used by God.

In spite of, or perhaps because of, Falwell's confidence that God will stay man's hand where the use of nuclear weapons is concerned, he reserved his choicest vituperation for advocates of disarmament.

...we [do not] have to march out in the streets with the peaceniks and the freezeniks, who are in a suicidal effort, a national suicidal effort to force our country into some unilateral disarmament that would place us at something less than parity in our ability to protect ourselves against the hammer and the sickle, Marxist-Leninists, who are set out to conquer the world.[8]

At the same time, he reserves a place for disarmament:

It is important that I state my earnest belief in the need for our government to negotiate for peace with the Soviet Union and other nations. We have a human responsibility to do all we can to seek sensible arms controls, eventual multilateral disarmament with impeccable inspection available to all parties involved, and so forth.[9]

Like other premillennialists before him, Falwell has struggled with the issue of choice and determinism. The sense of a cosmic timetable appears to foreclose the opportunity and the need for meaningful policy choices, but there remains the fear that however clear God's plan, it might in the end be sabotaged by human malice or error. That such an error might include accidental nuclear war, however, is a possibility Falwell fails to address. The danger instead lies in some form of Soviet nuclear blackmail.

Hal Lindsey takes a more audacious course, in which he lays out a highly detailed political chronology for the Tribulation period. Far from arguing that we need have no worries about nuclear war, Lindsey offers a succession of nuclear events, beyond anything in even the most pessimistic assessments of nuclear strategists. In three works, *The Late Great Planet Earth* (1970), *There's a New World Coming* (1973, revised 1984) and *The Rapture* (1983), Lindsey offers what is in effect a reinterpretation of the Book of Revelation in nuclear terms.

The Late Great Planet Earth has earned at least a footnote in publishing history. The 7,500,000 copies sold made it the largest-selling American non-fiction book of the 1970s.[10] On the basis of his reading of Revelation, Daniel, and Ezekiel, Lindsey presents an elaborate set of political, economic, and military predictions, including four separate nuclear episodes, of varying intensity, predicted with varying degrees of assurance. Like many other premillennialists, Lindsey believes a vast Asian—principally Chinese—army will advance on the Middle East in the "latter days." This "Asian horde" will kill one-third of the world's population, possibly with the use of nuclear weapons. The Chinese, however, will not be the only ones fighting in the region, for there will also be a confrontation between the European forces of Antichrist and a Russian military force, during which the former may employ tactical nuclear weapons. When the combat escalates, however, an exchange of nuclear missiles is possible.[11] Although Lindsey presents the battle of Armageddon as a land battle employing conventional weapons, albeit on a stupendous scale, he expects it to be accompanied by worldwide nuclear missile attacks in which "entire islands and mountains will be blown off the map" as the great cities of the world are destroyed.[12]

As chilling as is this scenario, it pales before the events described in Lindsey's 1973 work, *There's a New World Coming*. Predictions once made tentatively are now voiced with confidence and the number of nuclear attacks has at least doubled. More significantly, nuclear war now appears as the fulfillment of specific prophecies in the Book of Revelation, with as much attention given the aftereffects of detonations as on the immediate blast casualties. Thus, when Revelation's fourth seal is opened, the result is a global nuclear war in which between a fourth and a half of humanity is killed.[13] For the sake of internal consistency, the lower figure is presumably what Lindsey meant, given what is to come. The sixth seal will be accompanied by a nuclear exchange so massive that it will precipitate earthquakes along fault-lines that have not yet been discovered. The vehicles will be MIRVed ICBMs, some carrying "dirty" cobalt warheads to maximize radioactive contamination. The attack will throw up sufficient clouds of dust and debris to create a "nuclear winter."[14]

As Lindsey passes from the prophecies that are unsealed to those accompanied by angel trumpeters, additional nuclear holocausts appear. The first angel, for example, predicts a "massive nuclear attack much larger than the first one described in the sixth seal of Chapter 6" of Revelation. With the second angel, life in the sea is nearly destroyed by the underwater explosion of "super-thermonuclear weapons." The fourth angel brings darkness created by atmospheric post-attack dust clouds.[15] A limited nuclear strike accompanies the sixth angel as the Chinese army marches, and at this point Lindsey pauses to tally the casualties. One-fourth having been killed in the initial attacks, by a conservative measure, and others having succumbed to radiation poisoning, the pathetic survivors constitute two-thirds of the pre-Tribulation population. The Chinese then attack utilizing "some kind of mobilized ballistic missile launcher."[16]

Finally, Lindsey reaches the "seven bowls of wrath." The first is radiation sickness which produces "malignant...hideous sores." The second bowl brings the killing of marine life produced by "a tremendous nuclear exchange, or perhaps some unknown weapon that will be the result of the Stars [sic] Wars research...." The fourth bowl brings a rise in world temperature after nuclear explosions deplete the ozone layer.[17] Lindsey associates the bowls of wrath with Armageddon and "World War III," in the course of which nuclear attacks will severely damage Israel, the Soviet Union, and Eastern Europe. Much of the attack will be mounted by the Chinese, but the European forces of "Antichrist" will use tactical nuclear weapons. The pouring of the seventh bowl corresponds to the firing of all remaining nuclear missiles. "(E)very city in the world is going to be leveled," although it is unclear how many would still be habitable by the time this stage is reached.[18]

With the return of Christ and his saints and the inauguration of the millennium, the radioactive rubble will yield, according to Lindsey, to a thousand years of unparalleled peace and plenty. Then, following the final judgment, will come the greatest nuclear explosion of all, "when

God releases *all* the atoms in our earth and its surrounding universe."[19] Rather in the manner described by Jerry Falwell, God will disintegrate the world, although it seems rather an afterthought in light of the earlier rounds of destruction.

By the time Lindsey wrote *The Rapture* (1983), little remained to be said. The nuclear script is fundamentally as it was described in *There's a New World Coming*, save for a few refinements and clarifications. Thus the nuclear attacks associated with the opening of the sixth seal will involve a Soviet first-strike, followed by missile exchanges among the USSR, Europe, the United States, and China. Lindsey now joins these attacks to the prophecies of the first angel trumpeter rather than to a wholly new nuclear episode, for he concludes that the angel's promised devastation results from sixth seal fire storms which will burn the vegetation on a third of the earth's land areas. The marine attacks of the second trumpet now definitely result from "a great nuclear naval battle," which in addition to its effects on sea life destroy a third of all ships. The third trumpet, not initially associated with nuclear strife, is now identified with the radioactive contamination of "one-third of all the world's fresh water." By way of calculating the casualties, the opening of the seals and the sounding of the trumpets succeed in killing half the world's population within three years, primarily by nuclear weapons and their side-effects.[20]

Lindsey, understandably, does not have high expectations about arms control. Nuclear powers will never relinquish their arsenals, and in any case, thermonuclear war is ordained: "...I would love to be optimistic about a 'build-down' in the arms race, but my understanding of current events and Bible prophecy forces me to believe that just the opposite is true and that the world is indeed headed for grave times."[21] As in all premillennialist arguments, "the worse, the better." When Lindsey deals with American foreign policy, millennialist determinism is at constant war with political conservatism, the former implying that things must be as they are, the latter condemning the same developments as evidence of naivete and irresolution. The Soviet Union has a far more significant eschatological role to play than the United States according to Lindsey's view of history, but the USSR has risen to superpower status, he argues, only because of American mistakes. The SALT agreement was based on a "fatal assumption" that led the United States to "throw away" its superiority; America has "swallowed" Russian propaganda, placing it in "mortal danger." The resulting picture of "sickening clarity" will allow the Soviet Union and its satellites "to fulfill their predicted dreadful role in history."[22] Lindsey cannot conceal the thrill of prophecies confirmed even as he rails against those who purportedly made the fulfillment possible.

Falwell's and Lindsey's positions are superficially far apart, the one insisting nuclear destruction is at worst a far-distant event, while the other piles one missile exchange upon another. Yet they implicitly agree on one major issue: Ultimate responsibility for nuclear war is not held by human hands. If nuclear powers exercise restraint, it is only because the deity has other plans. Were nuclear war to break out, it would only be a fulfillment of a divine mandate. In either case, policymakers maintain only the most superficial appearance of control. Those who seek to minimize the risks through campaigns for arms control are misguided individuals who naively believe that human action can effect the flow of history.

Apocalyptic Symbols and Moral Order

Traditional religious accounts assigned the world's destruction to the intervention of supernatural forces. Nuclear weapons open the possibility that the same result can now be brought about by human accident, blundering, or self-destructiveness: "The destructive half of the divine power now makes its home in man: this much of deity is incarnate in mortal flesh." [23] As a result, God has seemingly lost the monopoly over the "end of the world." In addition, a nuclear conflict would inevitably kill or injure enormous numbers of innocent persons, including the inhabitants of non-belligerent states. The prospect of nuclear war thus constitutes a vast affront to conceptions of moral order which require that suffering be deserved.

The problem confronting religious fundamentalists is consequently twofold: On the one hand, they must assimilate nuclear weapons—the symbol of human destructive power—to a world-view in which human beings are subordinate to God; and, on the other, they must do so in a manner that reconciles the prospect of nuclear war with moral order. Nuclear weapons must be treated as an aspect of a divine plan whose outcome permits the ultimate triumph of good over evil. Falwell and Lindsey have attempted precisely such a reconceptualization.

They have done so in part by subtly altering the premillennialist use of "portents." Portents are events that function as symbols of the nearness of the present to some predicted apocalyptic future. Natural disasters constituted one of the major categories of portents in traditional premillennialist literature. [24] However, since the nineteenth century, human mastery over nature has deprived events such as earthquakes and volcanic eruptions of their former apocalyptic significance, and it is assumed that even where the natural world cannot be controlled, it can be predicted and understood. Hence scientific and technological advances have eroded the older link between natural phenomena and providence, in effect depriving millenarians of one of their major classes of signposts.

Accordingly, disproportionate weight has fallen upon the other traditional category of portents, war and political tumult. Contemporary dispensationalists such as Falwell and Lindsey have fastened upon three types of political events: conflict in the Middle East, especially involving Israel; conflict between the United States and the Soviet Union; and the development of larger and more powerful nuclear arsenals. Nuclear weapons have emerged in contemporary millenarian literature as a surrogate for natural disasters. The danger and imminence of nuclear war promises precisely the finality that premillennial doctrine requires, for unlike past conflicts, war may now occur with no credible opportunity for victory or reconstruction. No matter how stable the international environment may be in other respects, the presence of nuclear weapons insures that predictions of a climactic battle between good and evil will appear inevitable.

The linkage of international conflict with the battle between good and evil provides the other element in the new millenarian synthesis. Not only have portents been adjusted to the new politico-military reality, nuclear war has been transferred from the realm of accident to that of divine design. Falwell assures his audiences that if nuclear weapons are used, they will be employed with restraint; and that their presence is all but essential so that America is allowed to safely pursue its salvationist mission, gathering saved souls against the coming day of wrath. Lindsey advises his readers that nuclear war is inevitable, but that it will occur in times and places already predicted in scriptural literature, and that in consequence nuclear war is to be anticipated as a token of divine participation in earthly affairs.

Forecasts of nuclear war are dire predictions. Those who like Falwell and Lindsey believe in a pre-Tribulational Rapture, are in a peculiarly advantageous position with regard to such predictions, for they can promise safety to believers; the saved will be divinely rescued in the pre-Tribulational Rapture. In addition to the security that the Rapture provides, Falwell practices a more explicit form of denial.   He insists that no nuclear war will occur, and that nuclear arms are both necessary and effectively risk-free. On the matter of the potency of human action, he is inconsistent but not equivocal. The United States must defend itself from the Soviet Union, which implies that God's protection of America is not absolute. Those who press for disarmament place the

United States on the road to subjugation. In the area where human actions count—defense policy—their effect is pernicious, and in the area where human actions are superfluous—nuclear war—agitation for disarmament is unnecessary. Although God may not protect America from the Soviet Union, the deity will presumably protect the human race from destroying itself in an exchange of missiles. One can, according to Falwell, be justifiably anxious about the activities of "the peaceniks and the freezeniks." In some sense, their actions "count." But one need not lose sleep over the fear that "someone's going to push the button and destroy the planet." That decision, Falwell insists, only appears to be a human decision. Falwell thus represents a nearly pure example of a religious argument whose function is to deny the danger of nuclear war.

While Falwell exemplifies the position of deniers, Lindsey finds nuclear war overwhelmingly attractive. He too holds out the promise of a raptured rescue for the saved, but it is far more important to his argument than to Falwell's, for Lindsey's nuclear Tribulation leaves the world a depopulated desert. The lurid descriptions, in the style of supermarket tabloids, betray a fascination with the magnitude of the disasters. His description of the battle of Armageddon provides a representative example of Lindsey's genre style:

It's almost impossible for us to imagine the magnitude of what is predicted here. Just imagine—at least 300 million soldiers strung out across the entire Middle East and poised for the final mad act in man's most finely-developed art—war! The human waves of the East are pitted against the superior weaponry of the West. Then it happens—the final battle begins! The horrible carnage of the Valley of Armageddon... the indescribable clashes around Jerusalem and Judea.... No wonder John predicts that blood will stand to the horses' bridles for two hundred miles in the Jordan Valley![25]

Falwell's and Lindsey's writings are exemplars of a form of religious discourse that now occupies a seemingly secure niche in American popular culture, diffused by paperback racks, religious bookstores, and cable television in addition to churches themselves. Its volume suggests that large numbers find that it provides an at least intermittently persuasive picture of the world. This potential audience—one-fifth to two-fifths of the adult population[26]—may be assumed either to seek out such material to reinforce millenarian views they already hold or to modify their views as a result of exposure to dispensationalist doctrine.

A national survey conducted in 1984 found that 39% of the sample believed that "When the Bible predicts that the earth will be destroyed by fire, it's telling us that a nuclear war is inevitable." The number agreeing fell to 28% among college graduates but rose to 49% among persons earning less than $20,000. A significant minority (26%) believed that "In a nuclear war with the communists, our faith in God would ensure our survival." These beliefs became majority positions among those most prone to view the U.S-Soviet struggle as a clash of moral values. Among them, fully 67% identified nuclear war with Biblical prophecy, while 55% relied on God for survival.[27] Significantly similar views also appear to be held by at least some high policymakers.

When Harvard students asked Secretary of Defense Caspar Weinberger in 1982 about his views concerning the end of the world, the Secretary responded: "I have read the Book of Revelation and yes, I believe the world is going to end—by an act of God, I hope—but every day I think that time is running out. I worry that we will not have enough time to get strong enough to prevent nuclear war. . . . I think time is running out. . .but I have faith."[28] Far more widely publicized was the exchange between Ronald Reagan and Marvin Kalb of NBC during the second 1984 Presidential Debate. Surely one of the oddest exchanges ever to take place between a journalist and a sitting President, it began when Kalb asked, "Do you feel that we are now heading perhaps for some kind of nuclear Armageddon, and do you feel that this country and the world could survive that kind of calamity?" The President responded that "no one knows whether Armageddon. . .is 1,000 years away or the day after tomorrow" and "I have never seriously warned and said we must plan according to Armageddon." He did, however, acknowledge that he had had "philosophical discussions" about Biblical prophecies of Armageddon, and that according to "a number of theologians. . .the prophecies are coming together that portend that." The issue came up in the forum of a nationally televised debate in part because Reagan had made similar statements on and off the public record, some suggesting, at least to their auditors, more than merely "philosophical" implications.[29]

Neither the survey data nor the statements of officials can conclusively determine the effect this literature may have upon actual behavior. Millenarian logic suggests that the closer people believe themselves to be to the end-time, the less constrained they will feel to pursue ordinary routines, and in particular to engage in those behaviors that involve working toward goals remote in time. Much of human life—procreation and child-rearing, economic production not tied to immediate consumption, and the cultivation of interstate diplomacy—falls into this category and would thus be made contingent by millenarian imminence. Yet it is equally the case that notwithstanding the large audiences attracted by millenarian books and by the "electronic church," normal patterns of life have not been interrupted, save among exceedingly small survivalist coteries. How is it that devotees of millenarian literature find it possible to avoid or evade its behavioral implications?

Dispensational premillennialism is a structure of rationalization that seeks to remove the contradiction between unmerited suffering in nuclear war and belief in a morally ordered universe. On top of this structure of rationalization, however, a second structure must be erected in order to make it possible for those who hold dispensationalist views to continue the normal routines of life. This second structure of rationalization justifies the continuation of everyday life for rank-and-file dispensationalists, as well as the expansion of the institutional structure of dispensationalist churches, television programs, and publishing ventures. The latter are required by the need to "harvest" as many souls as possible prior to the Rapture and Tribulation, while the former may be explained away as temporary expedients. A.G. Mojtabai, in her lengthy interviews of dispensationalists in Amarillo, Texas, encountered this form of bridging explanation as in the following conversation with a fundamentalist minister:

"I believe in living as if the Lord is coming any day," he reasons. "Work like he were not coming for a thousand years."

"You carry life insurance?" I cannot refrain.

"Yes." Again, no problem. "In case the Lord tarries. Death could come. I want my wife to be provided for."

No contradiction at all: "When that trump sounds," he declares, "I'm going to take off like an astronaut!"[30]

Belief in the millennium's imminence would also seem to require abstention from ordinary political activity, as it did among American millenarians in the nineteenth century. Before Jimmy Carter first ran for the Presidency in 1976, fundamentalists exhibited unusually low voter turnouts.[31] Contemporary dispensationalists, however, have continued to mobilize politically,[32] and that, too, requires an additional layer of rationalization. Tim LaHaye has argued that without fundamentalist political activity, there will be a "pre-tribulation tribulation:"

...that is, the tribulation that will engulf this country if liberal humanists are permitted to take total control of our government...[and that] is neither predestined nor necessary.[33]

Yet it is unclear how the genuine Tribulation, which the saved may meet with equanimity, is to be distinguished from an inauthentic precursor.

This dilemma points to the increasingly troubling relationship dispensationalist millenarians have with the prediction of future events. Initially constructed to avoid the embarrassing falsification of predictions, dispensationalism now sees events as moving with rapidity towards the "latter days." Thus, on the one hand dispensationalists seize upon any political crisis that indicates the nearness of the Tribulation, while on the other they seek to avoid claims to know the precise timing of it and of the accompanying Rapture. Yet the rhetoric of "almost there but not quite" is difficult to maintain indefinitely, and claims of dispensationalist interpretive successes may enmesh millenarians in the kind of calamitous false predictions that destroyed the Millerite movement in the 1840s.[34]

Dispensationalists see themselves on an ill-defined temporal frontier between past mundane time for which ordinary human routines are appropriate and an oncoming sacred future during which the saved and unsaved will be irrevocably divided. For all its claims to exegetical precision and Biblical inerrancy, dispensationalists remain reluctant to specify in more exact terms the timing of the Tribulation and Rapture. Hence they insist upon imminence while maintaining and advocating traditional attitudes towards work, consumption, and other worldly activities. The logic of their argument, however, would appear to push them slowly but insistently toward greater rather than lesser predictive specificity, even at the risk of eventual disconfirmation.

The behavior deemed appropriate to the end-time is traditionally conceived in negative rather than positive terms—the avoidance of activities and obligations considered inappropriate or unnecessary. In addition, the divine timetable in which premillennialists believe holds a relatively small place for human agency, emphasizing instead the control of God over key historic processes: whatever is destined to happen, will happen, and since the Rapture-Tribulation-Second Coming-Millennium sequence is considered a historic terminous, its inauguration cannot be stopped.

This position has particularly important implications for nuclear war. Lindsey's writings and the genre he represents carry the danger that their predictions of a nuclear apocalypse may become a self-fulfilling prophecy. Although this fear attaches with particular force to the writings of those attracted to nuclear war, it also applies with only slightly less force to deniers such as Falwell. Falwell too promises rescue for the saved, who feel doubly protected, for they also confidently believe God will not permit nuclear war. If that is the case, human vigilance is unnecessary. The prospect of self-fulfilling nuclear prophecies has been widely noted among critics of the contemporary premillenarian position. Steven Kull suggests that images of destruction can have a determinative as well as a predictive meaning, as individuals seek to realize what they have been habituated to expect.[35]

While premillennialists disclaim any desire to "force the end" by precipitating the events they expect, they may establish a climate in which the expected is perceived as inevitable. "It needs little imagination to understand the consequences of such a belief, especially if held with deep conviction by politicians and the military who have the power to press the button and to execute the judgment thus prophesied and foreordained."[36] Actions otherwise viewed as in principle the product of reflection and choice may become subtly transformed into behavior that must occur, with only the details of timing left in doubt. The attitudes of premillennialists might be expected to add only a small measure of influence to the process by which policy outcomes are determined. Nonetheless, that process already contains ominously deterministic elements. The complex and cumbersome technology of nuclear deterrence leaves little enough room for genuine choice; warning times are short, intelligence often ambiguous, and decision capacity, such as it is, devolves upon a small number of individuals operating under conditions of great stress. Within such a setting, a predisposition to let events take a seemingly predestined course may have large and uncorrectable consequences. These consequences will be magnified further to the extent that a belief that God is the only actor with real control over events may have discouraged the development of possible mechanisms for control and prevention.

The psychological benefit premillennialists derive from their nuclear speculations is clear: Nuclear war is a massive affront to the belief that we live in a morally ordered universe where people "get what they deserve and deserve what they get."[37] Conceptions of just desert become a sham in a world where all may perish for the offenses or stupidity of a few. Premillennialist nuclear doctrine, whether espoused by a denier such as Falwell or an affirmer such as Lindsey, restore a sense of moral order for believers. Thus, "the atomic age and apocalypticism are made for each other," the former creating the anxieties which the latter claims to assuage.[38] It is surely no crime to minister psychological first-aid in dangerous times. However, to do so for a mass following through sophisticated media of communication introduces a potentially dangerous passivity and fatalism into precisely that area of policy consideration most in need of decisive control.

An earlier version of this paper—"Nuclear War and Millenarian Symbols"—was presented at the Annual Meeting of the Society for the Scientific Study of Religion in Savannah, Ga., October 25-27, 1985. For subsequent comments and suggestions I am particularly indebted to Ira Chernus, David Rapoport, Andrew G. Lang, and Timothy Weber.

Notes

[1] Norman Cohn *The Pursuit of the Millennium* (New York, 1970), 15.

[2] 1 Thessalonians 4: 16-17.

[3] Timothy P. Weber, *Living in the Shadow of the Second Coming,* (Grand Rapids, MI, 1983) 20-22. While believers in a pre-Tribulational Rapture dominate current premillennialist thought, a small minority of so-called "post-Tribulationists" believe the saved must endure the torments of the Tribulation along with everyone else. The logic of their position takes some post-Tribulationists into survivalism, the creation of remote, self-sufficient communities in which they hope to wait out the seven years of violence.

[4] *Los Angeles Times,* March 4, 1981.

[5] Jerry Falwell, *Nuclear War and the Second Coming of Jesus Christ* (Lynchburg, VA., 1983), 2, 4.

[6] Jerry Falwell, "Nuclear War and the Second Coming of Jesus Christ," cassette tapes (Lynchburg, Va., 1983).

[7] Ibid.

[8] Ibid.

[9] Falwell, *Nuclear War,* 2-3.

[10] *New York Times Book Review,* April 6, 1980, 27.

[11] Hal Lindsey, *The Late Great Planet Earth* (New York, reprinted 1973), 71.

[12] Ibid., 149-50, 153, 155.

[13] Hal Lindsey, *There's a New World Coming* (Eugene, Or., "updated" edition, 1984), 88.

[14] Ibid., 96-98.

[15] Ibid., 117-120.

[16] Ibid., 127-29.

[17] Ibid., 204-07.

[18] Ibid., 211-213.

[19] Ibid., 271.

[20] Hal Lindsey, *The Rapture: Truth or Consequences* (New York, 1983), 12, 13.14.

[21] Lindsey, *There's a New World Coming,* 119-211.

[22] Hal Lindsey, *The 1980's: Countdown to Armageddon* (New York, reprinted 1981), 76-77, 84-85.

[23] Charles H. Taylor, "Apocalyptic Power and Human Care," *The Yale Review* 73 (1984): 493-94.

[24] Michael Barkun, *Crucible of the Millennium: The Burned-over District of New York in the 1840s* (Syracuse, NY, 1986), 49-50.

[25] Lindsey, *There's a New World Coming,* 212-13.

26The issue of the size of American fundamentalism is conflicted and complex. The problems include distinguishing fundamentalists and evangelicals and distinguishing size and visibility. On the former, see James D. Hunter, "Operationalizing Evangelicalism: A Review, Critique and Proposal," *Sociological Analysis* 42 (1982): 363-72. On the latter, R. Lawrence Moore, "Insiders and Outsiders in American Historical Narrative and American History," *American Historical Review* 87 (1982): 390-412. A 1978 Gallup survey identified 19% of the population supporting key fundamentalist theological precepts, although a minority of those so responding were Catholics. "Religion in America," *The Gallup Report* 184 (1978).

27The Public Agenda Foundation, *Voter Options on Nuclear Arms Policy* (New York, 1984), 37, 40.

28*New York Times*, August 23, 1982, A14.

29*New York Times* October 23, 1984, A28.

30A.G. Mojtabai, *Blessed Assurance: At Home with the Bomb in Amarillo, Texas* (Boston, 1986), 153.

31Corwin Smidt, "Evangelicals versus Fundamentalists: An Analysis of the Political Characteristics and Importance of Two Major Religious Movements within American Politics," paper prepared for delivery at the Annual Meeting of the Midwest Political Science Association, Chicago, IL., April 20-23, 1983.

32The most recent example is the success achieved by "Pat" Robertson in utilizing fundamentalists to pursue delegates for the Republican Presidential nomination.

33Tim LaHaye, *The Battle for the Mind* (Old Tappan, N.J., 1980), 217-18.

34Weber, *Living in the Shadow*, 242.

35Steven Kull, "Nuclear Arms and the Desire for World Destruction," *Political Psychology* 4 (1983): 577-78.

36D.S. Russell, *Apocalyptic: Ancient and Modern* (Philadelphia, 1978), 64.

37Melvin J. Lerner, *The Belief in a Just World: A Fundamental Delusion* (New York, 1980).

38Weber, *Living in the Shadow*, 232.

Electronic Church: Fearsome or Folly?

Nick Thorndike

On a recent broadcast, Oral Roberts urged his television audience to remember the "God of a Second Chance." He offered a book he had written on the subject to anyone who would call a toll-free number listed on the TV screen. The call and the book would cost nothing to the viewer. Roberts must have considered the book an investment in his ministry. In his thirty or so years on television, Roberts may have reached more people than any president of the United States.

The Electronic Church has undoubtedly affected millions of Americans. Jerry Rifkin has said that "a close look at the evangelical communications network...should convince even the skeptic that it is the most important cultural force in America today."[1] Rifkin may be overstating the case, but he is right in pointing out the influence and significance of "video" religion. The religious organizations sponsored by Jerry Falwell, Oral Roberts, and others have continued to attract viewers year after year. Most people in America, positively or negatively, have felt the impact of the Electronic Church. What distresses many critics about the Church is that it offers little of substance to the viewing public. But the Electronic Church should not be feared as a huge and monstrous cultural phenomenon as some writers have supposed.[2] The Church has more human flaws than is apparent at first glance.

The history of the Electronic Church extends back to pioneer days, when revivals and "religious awakenings" were popular in America. Preachers (including Oral Roberts' father, Ellis) covered large stretches of land by horseback. They tried to convert people with sermons and preaching. Often they held religious services that attracted thousands. The roots of their religion grew from Pentacostalism and Methodism.[3] Ministers who came from these traditions stressed emotion over

174

Inside James Schuller's Crystal Cathedral. Let there be light.

Crystal Cathedral, California.

intellectualism. They hoped their audiences would experience a total conversion based on the heart.

Evangelical comes from the Greek *evangelion*, or evangel, meaning "good news." We mean here conservative Protestant Christians who follow very closely their theological tenets: inerrancy of the Bible, conversion, and the divinity of Jesus.

Evangelicals soon had a decisive hold on many TV and radio markets. As early as the 1920's, the Rev. R.R. Brown had created what he called the "World Radio Congregation." In 1934, Herbert W. Armstrong began the Radio Church of God which he later parlayed into a successful television ministry. The influence of the evangelicals, however, fluctuated throughout the years. They had to compete for radio and TV time with churches organized by the Federal Council of Christ Church and American Council of Churches ACC as well as with other religions groups. They also lost a valuable voice when William Jennings Bryan died after the Scopes trial in 1928.

We should remember that many broadcasters were simply interested in the form of these religious shows rather than in their content. The National Broadcasting Company established strict guidelines for broadcasting religious programs.[4] Evangelicals were probably used as much as they used their technical media. Having learned from their broadcasting experience, these ministers could branch out into other areas. But it is not true that they encountered no setbacks along the way. As a matter of fact, many ministries floundered; some today still have financial and technical problems.

The "electric Church" grew out of the frustrations and anxiety that the evangelicals experienced. They had definite views on public education, race relations, and religion which they wanted to publicize. They felt cast aside by a society that experimented with social liberalism under the Roosevelt and Truman administrations.

Evangelicals often became combative, rejecting innovations and ideas such as the theory of evolution. Their combativeness was, perhaps, a sign of their insecurity: Would they be heard by a society that seemed to be constantly changing? Many of their tactics left much to be desired. For instance, some evangelicals eagerly supported Senator McCarthy's campaigns against the "godless" communists.[5] However, evangelicals had the desire and right to broadcast their religion. Like many Americans, they had questions about what the ultimate value of life was and wanted to provide some answers.

What were their answers? And why do they hold to their convictions so strongly? Evangelicals engaged in broadcasting often seem smug and overconfident about their beliefs. For example, Jim Bakker, host of the *Praise the Lord* program, has said, "...my specific calling from God is to be a talk show host."[6] What motivates them?

Their message, simply stated, revolves around the Bible. The Bible, as the evangelicals know it, has all the answers to every human problem.

Preachers display the Bible prominently on their TV shows. Often they include Bibles as free gifts to viewers who watch their program. According to them, the gospel writers—Matthew, Mark, Luke, and John—received a direct revelation from God which led them to compose the scriptures. This testament binds all people together and must be believed in order for a person to be saved.

The difference between the evangelicals and other Christians is the intensity of their beliefs. Indeed, for many of the evangelicals, their beliefs become a compulsion. They revel in religious feeling. For instance, on many of his TV shows, Jimmy Swaggart often breaks down crying. He encourages the audience to share his tearful response. Other primetime preachers such as Oral Roberts include direct, personal appeals to the viewer during their programs.

The message which Jimmy Swaggart or Oral Roberts preaches may sound familiar enough. But what they apparently like about their version of Christianity is its simplicity and directness. No one needs much advanced training in order to understand it. The theology which the evangelicals conceive is the literal truth. While it may seem simplistic, the evangelicals' message applies to a diverse kind of audience which longs for answers and for spiritual guidance.

In many cases, the educated and "liberal" viewers simply do not respond to evangelical preaching. Although the public may receive much information on the Electronic Church through mail-ins, new reports, TV exposure, or contact with "sworn" believers, they might not have the desire to pursue their interest. The Electronic Church, on the surface, looks flat and one-dimensional. The theology of the Church loses its appeal; individuals remain unmoved.

"On air" appeals of many TV preachers for financial assistance may complicate matters. During the course of a religious program, we may hear dozens of pleas for cash to help fund projects sponsored by a particular organization. Surely, these appeals "turn off" audiences just as much as they turn on those who are already converted.

Long-time contributors must also feel a sense of frustration. Their donations never seem to be enough. Oral Roberts, for instance, constantly reminds viewers of how much money he needs. Roberts' pleading might spur some families to give even more cash, but others must wonder: "Is my $5 or $10 really a help? Does it do any good?" Oftentimes the TV preachers send free gifts if a person calls their religious organization or uses a prayer hot-line.

In view of this situation, some members of the Electronic Church consciously cultivate an aura of success, perhaps to attract an even larger audience. On his TV shows, the Rev. Robert Schuler includes various shots of the Crystal Cathedral from whence he preaches. The Cathedral and its parishioners seem scrubbed clean and perfect. Rev. Schuler's message emphasizes the Bible and Christian salvation, but it seems to whitewash many aspects of Christianity including the idea of sin.[7] He often does not discuss issues such as the growing number of homeless people in America. His sermons generally have little substance, outlining themes and thoughts that are fairly commonplace.

We cannot overlook the mass network of computer technologies which the Electronic Church has successfully employed. Most of the computers have been used to keep files on and to contact the viewers. While many people must feel impressed when they receive a computer-generated letter which is personally addressed to them, others must find such technical ploys meaningless. These correspondences may give the illusion that the minister or organization cares; however, they seem just as shallow to persons who are familiar with the marketing strategies which these ministries use.[8]

Undoubtedly, many of the strategies do work. Considering that the Electronic Church has continued to grow by leaps and bounds, one realizes that the primetime preachers have been successful. But often holes show through: Computers may make mistakes. Viewers may not enjoy receiving a letter which has their name misspelled. Technical glitches have been known to occur.[9] The question is really not "if," but "when" these computer technologies will no longer function.

The question, of course, arises: How do these preachers of the Gospel affect the Church? Is their influence a positive or negative one? What I am trying to suggest is that although the ministers on TV (and radio) have much at their disposal in terms of technology, theology, and personality, they also cause many people to doubt their mission. Many of the Electronic Church's chief exponents seem guided by self-interest rather than by God. Such a situation cannot have a good impact on Christianity. By emphasizing an approach to religion based on simplistic emotion and on "face value," the primetime preachers neglect the permanence and substance which a religion can provide. They emphasize a kind of "go-getter" morality that has nothing to do with religion or Christianity. They leave much by the wayside and have to dispense with traditions, including art and music, which do not fit onto the TV landscape.

In his *Electronic Giant,* Stewart Hoover argues that because of TV "we are in the midst of a revolution—a revolution in the way we communicate as a society."[10] Considering the "revolutionary" nature of the technical media, I must agree that the Electronic Church will probably change the way in which persons conceive of religion. Instead of a cultural-social milieu which binds people together, religion may become instead a technological version of "show and tell." The preachers might gain a respectability and prestige which they do not deserve. They may continue to stress quantity over quality, thereby denying much of what makes Christianity meaningful.

The Christian religion appeals to people because of its depth. We see it expressed in such painters as El Greco and Da Vinci. Composers ranging from Bach to Mozart use Christian themes in their music. Hollywood producers often have turned to the Bible, filming such epics as *The Robe* for audiences worldwide to enjoy. These traditions should not be suppressed. However, when I think of how superficial the TV preachers can be with their message of salvation, I worry about the shape into which Christianity will evolve. Will Christianity simply become a showpiece or curio, for acquisition by a limited number of people?

Another distressing change is the general political shift to the right in the United States. It is easy to believe that the TV preachers have contributed to this trend toward fundamentalism. The adherents of the Electronic Church often profess neoconservative or reactionary politics. Some ministers such as the Rev. Jerry Falwell have actively involved themselves in various political struggles. Others have made ignorant and potentially racist remarks about ethnic groups and minorities. Father Charles Coughlin in the 1940's was probably one of the most famous for broadcasting racist opinions.[11]

More moderate ministers such as Robert Schuler have provided something of a balance to the fanaticism and reactionism of a Jerry Falwell. But even Rev. Schuler boils his faith down to a few basic "fundamental" truths.[12] The religion which he preaches rests on creeds and belief statements rather than on any other kind of value system. Such an insistence on doctrine and belief does not bode well for those who conceive of Christianity differently. If those following the primetime preacher have their way, Christianity will remain a superficial relic based on Biblical literalism and strict adherence to doctrine.

We should also remember that in general men and men only control the Electronic Church. Evangelical preachers such as Aimee Semple McPherson, a popular woman minister during the 1940's, will not have any influence if current norms are not challenged. Women who feel a calling to the ministry may not receive the same treatment that men receive. Unless women gain more power within the Electronic Church, the church's ultraconservativism will surely cause it to self-destruct.

The more these evangelicals engage in politics, the more we should be watchful. Jeffrey Hadden in *Primetime Preachers* asks "what means a Rev. Falwell might employ in pursuit of his goals in America."[13] We should share Hadden's concern. The Electronic Church would be less of a worrisome development if its constituents didn't seem so intent in engaging in shady political work. In the film *Pink Triangles*, one Moral Majority administrator from Southern California is quoted as saying that he thinks capital punishment is appropriate for homosexuals. The Rev. Falwell's antipathy for alternative lifestyles is legendary. As long as the beliefs held by the Rev. Falwell do not become reality, the average citizen will not have to fear his rhetoric or influence on the political process.

Jeffrey Hadden wisely argues in *Primetime Preachers* that "there is no place in a Christian manner of political life for arrogance, manipulation, subterfuge, or holding others in contempt."[14] If religious groups— conservative or liberal—assert their superiority over other groups, then the public should act. Such attitudes are not in line with what Christianity generally teaches. The TV ministers violate their own principles when they engage in this kind of grandstanding.

We must believe that the Electronic Church has provided a space for religion in American life. Perhaps, countless Americans, especially older citizens, would not have a chance to participate in a congregation outside of one of the TV or radio ministries. The Electronic Church has given people the opportunity to debate the importance of religion in their lives. Without the presence of a Jimmy Swaggart or an Oral Roberts on TV each week, we might be forced to consider that Christianity had no sway over the American soul. But is it possible to create something better on TV? Can one produce a program which allows more room for introspection and meditation? That is the challenge. With success comes an awesomeness that might be fearsome. With failure ensues expensive and arrogant folly. We've had too much folly in the past. But never has it been so expensive!

Notes

[1]Jeffery Hadden, *Primetime Preachers*, (Reading, MA: Addison Wesley, Inc., 1983), p. 199.

[2]Perry Young in *God's Bullies* suggests just a thesis. See also Hadden, *Preachers*, p. 79.

[3]See Harold Ellens, *Models of Religious Broadcasting*, (Grand Rapids, MI: Eerdmans Press, 1974), p. 144.

[4]Ibid., p. 28.

[5]See Stewart Hoover, *The Electronic Giant*, (Elgin, IL: Brethren Press, 1982), p. 124.

[6]Hadden, *Preachers*, p. 32.

[7]Ibid., pp. 29-31.

[8]Hadden's discussion of the "illusion of intimacy" is relevant; see Hadden p. 63ff.

[9]See *Newsweek* article (January 6, 1986), p. 123, about a "glitch" which happened to the Rev. Falwell costing him over $500,000.

[10]Hoover, *Giant*, p. 12.

[11]See Hadden, *Preachers*, pp. 192-193.

[12]Ibid., pp. 29-31.

[13]Hadden, *Preachers*, p. 134ff.

[14]Ibid., p. 171.

The Rape of the Vulnerable

Ray B. Browne

The Holy Wars that have broken out among the American merchants of religion in the early 1987s reveal much about the nature of these purveyors of religious fervor as well as the culture in which they grow and prosper—as well as over-extend and fail.

Religion and religious fervor and activities are not the sole product but they may be one of the domains of democracy. Religious fervor is likely to follow the vagaries of capitalism, feeding on the same drives that fuel unbridled and unchecked capitalism—wealth, lust, greed and power—and frequently fall as capitalism gets out of control—as the Stock Market seemed to be in early 1987—and pays the price for its unbridled grab for the so-called fruits of capitalism.

The nature of the robber barons, as they once were called, by and large has been to grab for power and wealth among themselves, frequently leaving alone the small investor who does not represent enough wealth for the robber baron to bother with. But the nature of the religion merchants is to prey more on the poor than the rich, the vulnerable than the strong. In seeking small but steady contributors, the religion merchants, while getting much of their contributions from the steady middle-class which constitutes a steady source of wealth, has two fields open to them where the income, though perhaps not as large and steady, is sure. These two are the young and the old, both classes vulnerable to the honey-tongue blandishments which work through idealism and fear, the former being particularly the province of the young, the latter particularly the dread of the old.

The young have proved an especially fruitful field in the last decade. Perhaps the reasons can easily be found. President Reagan's attempt through the years to put prayer back into the schools is an effort to breach the gap established by the U.S. Constitution to keep church and state separate. Reagan's proposal to put the church back into the state shows obvious contempt for the Constitution and demonstrates to school children—public school and college and university—that the gap between the two can and should be breached, and they are happy to try.

This attitude reveals, among other things, a weakness in American culture. Throughout history, a culture with goals, with purposes in life, with things to do is ordinarily a culture with people less interested in themselves than in the world around them. Call it materialism, pragmatism, call it interest in the world, but such an attitude tends to keep people's minds off the warts of their own lives and outside themselves. The people tend therefore to be mentally more stable and healthier.

On the contrary, the culture and society that seems to be without goals, without outside motivation and reasons for being tends to get worried over the fate of the individuals, to be more concerned with the spirit and heart of the individual than with society and history.

The causes of such malaise lie deep. Perhaps one of them is a natural consequence of history and national growth. Apparently after two hundred years of generally unrestricted development and growth the United States has run out of frontier and open territory for development and has had to stop to take a breather, to regroup for further development, or to stagnate. Whatever the future movement, such a halt in development undoubtedly causes some concern among the young about their future. When they get scared, they turn to what people have always turned to in time of stress, religion and ritual of one kind or another. They thus become easy prey for the person in the business of peddling religion, whose product is ritual and promises security.

Another cause of the current malaise in American life is obviously education. In the past American education has been empirical or generally pragmatic. With enough of the ideal to keep the head of individuals up and the eyes looking toward the sky. Now, in the middle of the 1980s, the young and educable have found that the education of their fathers and mothers is not enough for them, not enough to prepare them psychologically or vocationally for the future. Disquieted, they are easy prey for the merchant of religion.

So God has gone back to school, if not in the form of instructor then surely as companion to the thinking students who carry with them easy susceptibility in their intellectual baggage. According to *Newsweek's On-Campus* (Nov. 1986), Velma Ferrell, adviser to the Baptist Student Union at Duke University, said, "There is a desire to have somebody telling you what to do, whether it be God or President Reagan." Apparently the magnitude of the fears of current life are too large for parents or professors to solve: so the young are going to the highest authority.

The natural herding instincts of students, when aroused, insist that they be a conservative and conserved member of a larger group, and religion provides the magnitude needed. *Newsweek's On-Campus*, again, quoted a representation of this herd-instinct in its excerpt from a recent Brown University prayer meeting: "We praise you for the fervency you've given us and ask you to increase it. Start a fire burning. There's nothing we desire more than for God to sweep across this campus." The same issue of the magazine pointed out another fruit of the religious fervor— an ethnic identity where people find their own roots and bush growth, a seeking, dangerously, which can lead to bigotry and blindness.*Newsweek's On-Campus*, again quoted Rabbi Marc Gopin, adviser to the Orthodox Jewish community at Brandeis University as saying, "People are clinging an inordinate amount to ethnic identification and not enough to spiritual ideals." Students see and worship the tree but not the forest; the particular but not the general. According to Gopin, "Say anything about Israel and people start screaming; say anything about God and people shrug their shoulders." Any group that can see outside its own boundaries recognize that there is danger in such narrow ethnicity.

So students are vulnerable in putting vague mysticism, and good intentions ahead of common sense driven by observations and practicality. They drive with all the strength and potential damage at their command, wholly committed.

Older people are likewise vulnerable for almost the same reasons. They are weighed down by the problems of the world, many of which they could not correct in their active years and for which they may feel responsible. But mainly they seem to be lonely in their daily life and frightened by their short future. Preachers may talk excitedly about the glories of the life after death and about how much they yearn to get to heaven and start enjoying the physical and spiritual delights of the place, but generally they are not eager to change locations. Even Oral Roberts, whose position in the hierarchy of heaven is presumably well established, looked upon God's threat to call him "home" unless he raised $8 million to revitalize his medical college at Oral Roberts University as more of a punishment than a reward, and he was not happy to make the switch from earth's vale of tears to heaven's streets of gold. So the vulnerable elderly give money that they could more properly spend on themselves to support the wealthy churches which threaten them if they don't support the churches and promise them consolation if they do. Little wonder that the elderly give up the necessities of their lives for the promised certainties of the after-life.

Along with the cultural uncertainties that weaken the fabric and faith of our daily lives, there is another very real aspect of life that religion merchants have always railed against and occasionally dallied in—sex. It is easy to see why. Psychologists have demonstrated that the drives of sex and religion are not unrelated—both develop fervor, for example— and one might well develop along with the other. Both have a common drive in power. Power over evil and one's self and power over one of the great drives of mankind, sex, which is often called the power of Satan. Often people in the religion business get caught up in the Satan of sex. In America, the witchcraft of early Salem has often been ascribed to the puberty awakening of the girls of the village. Nathaniel Hawthrone depicted vividly the weakness of the flesh when in *The Scarlet Letter* he had the Reverend Arthur Dimmesdale fall prey to the physical attractions of Hester Prynne. Hester Prynne was forced to wear the scarlet "A" on her bosom for Adulteress, but Dimmesdale was destroyed by his own sense of guilt. At a much later time, Sinclair Lewis pointed out in his novel *Elmer Gantry* that one reason preachers liked their job so much was that it supplied them with the finer things of life: chicken to eat and ladies' knees to look at every Sunday. There are also other perks.

And it is the other perks that have dragged real-life ministers of God into trouble throughout America's history. The Rev. Henry Ward Beecher, called in the years before the Civil War, "the greatest preacher since Saint Paul," and a preacher who earned the unheard-of salary of $40,000 a year, was one of the early ministers who apparently dallied with female members of his congregation. Aimee Semple McPherson, flamboyant, attractive and somewhat erratic Los Angeles evangelical preacher, wore her low-cut flowing white gowns and charmed her audience, until she disappeared one afternoon in May, 1926, with one of her employees. Sex was the downfall of Billy James Hargis in 1976, when a magazine reported that Hargis was enjoying the pleasures of this world with both male and female students. It has been observed that preachers, especially young power-houses on television, seem to be sex-symbols; it is little wonder that sometimes they give in to their fatal flaw and stoop to folly.

Such was the great crescendo of noise that has recently shaken the televangelism business to the base of its golden feet. And the heaven-shaking event of the revelation of sexual irregularities among God's (self-) anointed has brought into (at least temporary) question the whole business of selling God through the media and with powerful gusto.

The crisis was precipitated when it was revealed that Jim Bakker, husband of Tammy Faye Bakker, and head of the television show PTL ("Praise the Lord," or as some have said less respectfully, "Pass the Loot") had had a one-night tryst with a former church secretary named Jessica Hahn and had subsequently paid her blackmail. Many people (especially the large number of preachers who could take sides in this *cause celebre*) felt that the devil in the drama was Jimmy Swaggart, an evangelist based in Louisiana, who was happy to exploit the discomfort of the Bakker family. Oral Roberts denounced Swaggart, as did Robert Schuller, from his $18 million Crystal Cathedral in California. Jerry Falwell, who took over the PTL when Bakker resigned, and Pat Robertson, flexing his muscles to become a serious contender for the Presidency of the United States, both played the issue down the middle, seeing opportunity in the situation to clean house and improve the act.

Who, then, are today's televangelists and who their audience? In both cases the answers are fairly clear. The preachers are generally people with poor and impoverished backgrounds who had to overcome many privations to succeed in this land of opportunity. Frustrated in other directions, these people saw big bucks in peddling religion and, apparently with the sincerest beliefs in their product, turned their emotions into big business. And their business and profits are indeed large. Before their fall, the Bakkers had the PTL Organization with a reported $129 million annual revenues; included in their empire was the 2,300-acre theme park Heritage USA in Ft. Mill, S.C. Jimmy Swaggart's weekly "Jimmy Swaggart Hour" plays in more than 2 million households; his revenues reached $142 million in 1986. Robert Schuller reaches a claimed 1.7 million weekly with his Reformed Church in America; his 12-story Crystal Cathedral cost $18 million. Jerry Falwell's "Old Time Gospel Hour" is presumably watched by 547,000 weekly; his income in 1986 was reportedly $73.5 million including that from the Liberty Broadcasting Network and Liberty University. Pat Robertson presumably reaches 468,000 with his daily "700 Club" broadcast; he apparently had an income from his Christian Broadcasting Network of $129 million in 1986. The Dean of them all, Oral Roberts, a Pentecostal minister, has outclassed all his competitors, perhaps. His weekly broadcasts are supposed to reach 1.1 million households. His earthly assets include the City of Faith medical center, Oral Roberts University and religious enterprises in seven countries. There is no way to assess the personal wealth of these individuals, since they will not reveal what they claim are their modest salaries nor the numerous and wealthy perks that come as a part of their positions, including lavish homes, the finest in transportation, and perks for the immediate scions of these servants of God. But it has come to light that the Bakkers' annual salary before the Fall was $1.6 million.

Other than the young and the old, who are the people who support these ministers? Mainly, they are people just like the ministers, with poor and stress-strewn backgrounds, who see in the ministers what they wish they themselves could accomplish. According to Jeffrey Hadden, University of Virginia sociologist and coauthor of the study of such ministers *Prime Time Preachers,* as reported in *Newsweek,* April 6, 1987, "The people who like and follow them see them as real human beings who are 'like me and have problems like me, but are more successful'." In other words, the audience, who are perennial television watchers and who might be just too tired to get up and turn the TV dial, seem to be engaged in a kind of double-dupe. They are willing to support the duping of the American public because by doing that these people are getting back at a society that has not been as kind and beneficial to them as it should have been. They are willing to use God to get back at people and life.

Is the whole gang sincere? Are the televangelists sincere? and are the supporters sincere? The question and value of sincerity seems a charade. Tammy Faye Bakker is surely sincere because she has worried her problems through before accepting and feeling comfortable with them. For example, Tammy is quite free to tell how she first tried cosmetics, liked them but expected to be struck by lightning for using them. But God told her that it was perfectly all right for her to use cosmetics. Because of this Godly approval, Tammy then started manufacturing and selling cosmetics—undoubtedly dedicating the profits of the sales to the glorification of God, the Great Franchiser (apparently God is female, as novelist Dr. Andrew Greeley insists, and therefore understands the need of women to use and buy cosmetics). Tammy has also lately been addicted to prescription drugs and has tried to break the addiction. Is Jim Bakker sincere? He and Tammy Faye have always been open with the public. For example, their marital crisis in the early 1980s was a public affair, a soap opera that people enjoyed and forgave. Now he has been forced to admit the public into the affairs of his "sexual encounter," his admitted fling into infidelity. He has suffered the agony of the sinner. But being the self-appointed spokesman for the Divine, Jim now reports that God has forgiven him his transgression. According to *Newsweek,* April 6, 1987, psychologist and PTL family member Fred Gross revealed to Bakker's PTL club the circumstances by which young Jim received forgiveness: "He was sobbing. He was shaking so violently

I had to hold him. In 10 minutes we were on the floor. His face was buried in the carpet. He was sobbing and kicking and screaming.... If there has ever been a release, that was a release." Some people might think that such actions were more befitting a child's temper tantrum than a forgiveness by God, but apparently not. Like God, Bakker's vast following seem also prepared to forgive him, as they would forgive themselves. But Jerry Falwell, with his eye on either the bounties of the ministry or on the Great Bookkeeper, is less quick to forgive. "The ministry of God is a great responsibility," he is reported in *Newsweek*, April 6, 1987, to have said: "You don't get two shots at it." But as sociologist Todd Gitlin (reported by Mike Duffy of Knight-Ridder Services) said. "If you can be born twice, why not a third time?" If God gives franchises to every poor soul who claims a second birth, why not renew the franchise if the franchisee will simply clean up his act? That makes good business sense.

If there were drama in the Jim and Tammy Faye affair, there was even more in the Oral Roberts Ordeal, which was running at the same time in a different theater across the country. The Bakker affair was indeed truly soap opera. And the actors may still have a future. Mike Duffy, cited above, reported that sociologist Todd Gitlin said: "If they can't get back on the PTL show, maybe they can guest star on 'Dynasty'." But Oral Robert's drama was Faustian in every way. Roberts apparently had unconsciously mortgaged his soul to a greedy and lonely God who was going to take him "home" to Heaven if he did not start immediately doing much more good in this lowly world, this time in the form of an $8 million enhancement of his hospital services. Thus there began a mortal tussle between the supernatural desires of God and the very material wishes of the materialistically wealthy citizens of America for the body and soul of God's servant. The stakes could hardly have been higher. The richest nation in the world vs. God!

Observant people might have noticed that this country is overrun with hospital beds that cannot be filled, that Oral's enhancement of God through the hospital was merely the fattening of his own ego. And wags might have well have said that God could not be so lonely that he wanted to enrich his life prematurely with the presence of Oral. But the contributions poured in, despite the fact that many media outlets, the public in general and even fellow evangelists, probably because of sheer envy at the magnitude of the gulling, decried Roberts' threat of being snatched from the earth unless his devout public dug even deeper into their pockets and found money to keep him among us. They might have observed that it would be far cheaper for them if Oral went on to Heaven where apparently the streets are already paved with gold. But Roberts finally raised his $8 million, the last $1.4 coming from a man who had raised his money on dog racing. But money raised through gambling interests can easily be laundered and made appropriate for God's work.

What are the future of the televangelists after these major crises? Will they continue to prosper, to prey on the weak and vulnerable, or have the Roberts-Bakker affairs shamed them, tainted this kind of huckstering in religion, and lowed the value of their stock on the Heavenly Stock Exchange? If the explosions are merely part of a Great Religious Franchise War, a battle not dissimilar from say that between fast food outlets, then maybe some scheme may be devised that will recover the ground that may or may not have been lost by the shame of Oral Roberts' gulling the public about their buying his salvation from death or the naivete of a young man who discovered that sexual desires have very little conscience or even religious probity. Apparently God is not indeed on 24-hour vigil.

But how long will the public be gulled? Probably as long as the public does not have some definite purpose in mind, some national and personal goal that will pull them out of themselves and give them something serious and worthwhile to occupy their time. God should be conceived of as big and generous, not as small and petty. There must be some question about whether God is really concerned over whether Tammy uses cosmetics or not. Perhaps that is within the purview of her beauty operator and dermatologist. God surely would not want to interfere with free enterprise.

The overriding question is what are the characteristics of the culture in which those people work. Kind and charitable, long-suffering and gullible—those are not necessarily undesirable traits of our democratic society. But there are perhaps grounds and room for some kind of different attitude toward those religious robber barons who may be seducing the innocent and vulnerable, and with the understanding and even the approval of the people who ought to know better. There is, after all, more to society than the ego gratification of those who are serving themselves when they call themselves the servants of God.

Selected Bibliography

Allen, Robert J. "Catholic Social Doctrine in National Network Catholic Television Programs in the U.S., 1951-68." Ph.D. dissertation, New York University, 1972.

Anderson, Gerald H. and Stransky, Thomas F. *Evangelization* (New York: Paulist Press, 1975).

Armstrong, Ben. *The Electric Church* (Nashville: Thomas Nelson, 1979).

Attfield, Robin. *God and the Secular* (Cardiff: University College Cardiff Press, 1978).

Bachman, John W. *The Church in the World of Radio-Television* (New York Association Press, 1960).

Barna, George and McKay, William Paul. *Vital Signs: Emerging Social Trends and the Future of American Christianity* (Westchester, Ill.: Crossway Books, 1984).

Barr, James. *Fundamentalism* (Philadelphia: The Westminister Press, 1977).

Benson, Dennis. *Electric Evangelism* (Nashville: Abingdon, 1973).

Berger, Peter and Neuhaus, Richard, eds. *Against the World, For the World* (New York: The Seabury Press, 1976).

Bestic, Alan. *Praise the Lord and Pass the Contribution* (London: Cassell, 1971).

Bethell, Tom. "The Common Man and the Electric Church." *Harpers*, (April 1978): 86-90.

Bloesch, Donald, *Essentials of Evangelical Theology: God, Authority, Salvation.* Vol. I, 1978. *Life, Ministry and Hope*, Vol. II, 1979 (New York: Harper & Row).

Boles, John B. *The Great Revival, 1787-1805: The Origins of the Southern Evangelical Mind* (Lexington: University of Kentucky Press, 1972).

Bruce, Dickson D., Jr. *And They All Sang Hallelujah: Plain-Folk Camp Meeting Religion, 1800-1845* (Knoxville: University of Tennessee Press, 1974).

Buddenbaum, Judith M. "The Audience for Religious Television Programs." M.A. thesis, Indiana University, 1979.

Christ, Carol and Plaskow, Judith. *Womanspirit Rising* (New York: Harper & Row, 1979).

Clabaugh, Gary K. *The Protestant Fundamentalists* (Chicago: Nelson-Hall, 1974).

Coleman, Richard. *Issues of Theological Warfare: Evangelicals and Liberals* (Grand Rapids, Michigan: Eerdmans, 1972).

Cross, Whitney R. *The Burned-Over District: The Social and Intellectual History of Enthusiastic Religion in Western New York, 1800-1850* (New York: Harper, 1965).

Daly, Mary. *The Church and the Second Sex* (New York: Harper & Row, 1968).

———. *Beyond God the Father: Toward a Philosophy of Women's Liberation* (Boston: Beacon Press, 1973).

———. *Gyn/Ecology: The Metaethics of Radical Feminism* (Boston: Beacon Press, 1978).

191

Diamond, Edwin and Bates, Stephen. *The Spot: The Rise of Political Advertising On Television* (Cambridge: MIT Press, 1984).

Dollar, George W. *A History of Fundamentalism in America* (Greenville, S.C.: Bob Jones University Press, 1973).

Douglas, Ann. *The Feminization of American Culture* (New York: Knopf. 1977).

Dumoulin, Heinrich. *A History of Zen Buddhism* (Boston: Beacon Press, 1969).

Dussel, Ennique. *Ethics and the Theology of Liberation* (Mary Knoll: Orbis Books, 1978).

Edwards, George R. *Gay/Lesbian Liberation: A Biblical Perspective* (New York: Pilgrim Press, 1984).

Ellwood, Robert S., Jr. *Alternate Altars: Unconventional and Eastern Spirituality in America* (Chicago: University of Chicago Press, 1979).

Engel, James F. *Contemporary Christian Communications* (Nashville: Thomas Nelson, 1979).

Falwell, Jerry, ed. *The Fundamentalist Phenomenon* (Garden City: Doubleday, 1981).

Fern, Dean William. *Contemporary American Theologies: A Critical Study* (New York: Seabury Press, 1981).

————. *Contemporary American Theologies II: A Book of Readings* (New York: Seabury, 1982).

Finney, James B. *Autobiography of James B. Finney; or, Pioneer Life in the West*, ed. W.P. Strickland. (Cincinnati: Methodist Book Concern, 1853).

Flowers, Ronald B. *Religion in Strange Times: The 1960s and 1970s* (Macon: Mercer University Press, 1984).

Fishwick, Marshall W., editor. *The Hero in Transition* (Bowling Green: Popular Press, 1983).

————. *Common Culture and the Great Tradition* (Westport: Greenwood Press, 1984).

————. *The Seven Pillars of Popular Culture* (Westport: Greenwood Press, 1985).

Frank, Ronald E., and Greenberg, Marshall G. *The Public's Use of Television: Who Watches and Why* (Beverly Hills: Sage Publications, 1980).

Friendly, Fred W. *Due to Circumstances Beyond Our Control* (New York: Vintage Books, 1968).

Geertz, Clifford. *The Interpretation of Cultures* (New York: Basic Books, 1973).

Gerbner, George, with Kathleen Connoly. "Television as New Religion." *New Catholic World* (May/April 1978): 52-56.

Goethals, Gregor. *The TV Ritual: Worship at the Video Altar* (Boston: Beacon Press, 1981).

Hamilton, Neill Quinn. *Recovery of the Protestant Adventure* (New York: Seabury, 1981).

Handy, Robert E. *A Christian America: Protestant Hopes and Historical Realities* (New York: Oxford, 1984).

Henry, Carl F.H. *Evangelical Responsibility in Contemporary Theology* (Grand Rapids, Michigan: Eerdmans, 1957).

Henry, Carl F.H. *Basic Christian Doctrines* (New York: Holt, Rinehart & Winston, 1962).

Henry, Carl F.H. *Evangelicals in Search of Identity* (Waco, Texas: Word Books, 1976).

Henry, Carl F.H. *God, Revelation and Authority: God Who Speaks and Shows* 2 vols., 1976. vols. 3 and 4. (Waco, Texas: Word Books, 1979).

Herberg, Will. *Protestant-Catholic-Jew: An Essay in American Religious Sociology* (New York: Doubleday, 1955).

Hofstadter, Richard. *The Paranoid Style in American Politics* (New York: Random House, 1965).

Hoge, Dean and Roozen, David. *Understanding Church Growth and Decline, 1950-78* (New York: Pilgrim Press, 1979).

Holt, B. Russell, "Superbowl Christianity." *Ministry* (May 1980): 19.

Hoover, Stewart M. *The Electronic Giant: A Critique of the Telecommunications Revolution from a Christian Perspective* (Elgin: The Brethen Press, 1982).

Horsfield, Peter G. *Religious Television: The American Experience* (London: Longman, 1984).

Jewett, Robert, and Lawrence, John Shelton. *The American Monomyth* (New York: Doubleday, 1977).

Johnson, Charles A. *The Frontier Camp Meeting: Religion's Harvest Time* (Dallas: Southern Methodist University Press, 1955).

Judah, J. Stillson. *Hare Krishna and the Counterculture* (New York: John Wiley and Sons, 1974).

Kahle, Roger. *Religion and Network Television*, Unpublished M.A. thesis, (Columbia University, 1970).

Kelley, Dean M. *Why Conservative Churches Are Growing* (New York: Harper & Row, 1972).

King, Martin Luther, Jr. *Why We Can't Wait* (New York: New American Library, 1964).

Kuhns, William. *The Electronic Gospel* (New York: Herder and Herder, 1969).

Kung, Hans. *On Being a Christian* (New York: Doubleday, 1976).

La Barre, Weston. *They Shall Take Up Serpents* (Minneapolis: University of Minnesota Press, 1962).

Latourette, Kenneth Scott. *A History of the Expansion of Christianity*, 6 vols. (New York: Paternoster Press, 1971).

Le Bon, Gustave. *La Psychologie des Foules* (Paris: Presses Universitaires de France, 1973).

Lecky, Robert and Wright, Elliott. *Black Manifesto: Religion, Facism, and Reparations* (New York: Sheed and Ward, 1969).

Lewis, David L. *King: A Biography* (Urbana: University of Illinois Press, 1978).

Liebman, Robert, and Wuthnow, Robert. *The New Christian Right* (New York: Aldine, 1983).

McFague, Sallie. *Metaphorical Theology: Models of God in Religious Language* (Philadelphia: Fortress Press, 1982).

Mann, James, with Sarah Peterson. "Preachers in Politics: Decisive Force in '80?" *U.S. News and World Report* (September 15, 1980): 24-26.

Marsden, George. *Fundamentalism and American Culture: The Shaping of Twentieth Century Evangelicalism* (New York: Oxford University Press, 1981).

Marty, Martin. "The Electronic Church." *Missouri in Perspective* (March 27, 1978):5.

_____ *The Improper Opinion: Mass Media and the Christian Faith*, (Philadelphia: Westminister Press, 1961).

_____ *"The Invisible Religion."* *The Presbyterian Survey* (May 1979): 13.

_____ *A Nation of Behaviors* (Chicago: University of Chicago Press, 1976).

Pilgrims in their Own Land: 500 Years of American Religion (New York: Little Brown, 1984).

Mavity, Nancy Barr. *Sister Aimee* (New York: Doubleday Doran, 1931).

Mehta, Gita. *Karma Cola: Marketing the Mystic East* (New York: Simon and Schuster, 1979).

Merton, Thomas. *Mystics and Zen Masters* (New York: Dell Publishing Co., 1961).

Monaco, James. *Celebrity: The Media as Image Maker* (New York: Dell, 1978).

Morris, James. *The Preachers* (New York: St. Martin's, 1973).

Moseley, James G. *A Cultural History of Religion in America* (Westport: Greenwood Press, 1981).

Needleman, Jacob. *The New Religions* (New York: Doubleday, 1970).

——— *A Sense of the Cosmos: The Encounter of Modern Science and Ancient Truth* (New York: Doubleday, 1975).

Nelson, John Wiley. *Your God is Alive and Well and Appearing in Popular Culture*

Niebuhr, H. Richard. *Christ and Culture* (New York: Harper and Row, 1951).

Northtrop, F.S.C. *The Meeting of East and West: An Inquiry Concerning World Understanding* (New York: Macmillan, 1944).

Novak, Michael. *All the Catholic People* (New York: Herder and Herder, 1971).

Osborn, Ronald E. *The Spirit of American Christianity* (New York: Harper & Bros., 1958).

Owens, Virginia Stem. *The Total Image or Selling Jesus in the Modern Age* (Grand Rapids: Eerdmans, 1980).

Panikkar, Raimundo. *The Intra-Religious Dialogue* (New York: Paulist Press, 1978).

Park, Jeff. "PTL Encounters the FCC: Truthful Probe or Witch Hunt?" *Action* (March 1980): 10-14.

Pavols, Andrew J. *The Cult Experience* (Westport: Greenwood Press, 1982).

Peel, Robert. *Christian Science: Its Encounter with American Culture* (New York: Henry Holt, 1958).

Peterson, J.W. *Those Curious New Cults* (New Haven: Keats, 1975).

Phy, Allene Stuart. *The Bible and Popular Culture in America* (Philadelphia: Fortress Press, 1984).

Pierard, Richard V. *The Unequal Yoke: Evangelical Christianity and Political Conservatism* (New York: J. P. Lippincott, 1970).

Pollock, John. *Moody: The Biography* (Chicago: Moody Press, 1983).

Porterfield, Amanda. *Feminine Spirituality in America: From Sarah Edwards to Martha Graham* (Philadelphia: Temple University Press, 1980).

Quebedeaux, Richard. *The Young Evangelicals: Revolution in Orthodoxy* (New York: Harper & Row, 1974).

——— *The New Charismatics: The Origins, Development and Significance of Neo-Pentecostalism* (New York: Doubleday, 1976).

——— *The Worldly Evangelicals* (New York: Harper & Row. 1978).

Ranaghan, K. et D. *Le Retour de l'Esprit* (Paris: Les Editions du Cert, 1972).

Raschke, Carl. *The Interruption of Eternity: Modern Gnosticism and the Origins of the New Religious Consciousness* (Chicago: Nelson-Hall, 1980).

Real, Michael R. *Mass-Mediated Culture* (Englewood Cliffs, N.J.: Prentice-Hall, 1977).

Rockefeller Foundation Conference Report. *The Religion Beat: The Reporting of Religion in the Media* (New York: Rockefeller Foundation, 1981).

Rogers, Jack. *Confessions of a Conservative Evangelical* (Philadelphia: The Westminister Press, 1974).

———.ed. *Biblical Authority* (Waco, Texas: Word Books, 1977).

Ruether, Rosemary, ed. *Liberation Theology* (New York: Paulist Press, 1972).

——— and McLaughlin, Eleanor. *Women of Spirit: Female Leadership in the Jewish and Christian Traditions* (New York: Simon and Schuster, 1979).

Russell, Charles Allyn. *Voices of American Fundamentalism: Seven Biographical Studies* (Philadelphia, Westminister, 1976).

Ryan, Michael D. *The Contemporary Explosion of Theology* (Metuchen, N.J.: Scarecrow Press, 1975).

Sabato, Larry J. "Mailing for Dollars," in *Psychology Today*, vol. 18, no. 10, October 1984, pp. 38-52.

_____ *PAC Power: Inside the World of Political Action Committees* (New York: W.W. Morton, 1984).

_____ *The Rise of the Political Consultants* (New York: Basic Books, 1982).

Salisbury, W. Seward. *Religion in American Culture* (Homewood, Ill.: Dorsey Press, 1964).

Sandeen, Ernest R. *The Roots of Fundamentalism: British and American Millenarianism, 1800-1930* (Chicago: University of Chicago Press, 1970).

Scharpff, Paulus. *Geschichte der Evangelisation* (Basel: Brunnen-Verlag, 1964).

Schneider, Michael. *Neurose und Klassenkampf* (Towohlt, Germany, 1973).

Segundo, Juan Luis. *Our Idea of God, Vol. 3* Translated by John Drury (Maryknoll, New York: Orbis Books, 1974).

Segundo, Juan Luis. *Liberation of Theology* (Maryknoll, New York: Orbis Books, 1976).

Sheen, Fulton J. *Treasures in Clay* (New York: Doubleday, 1980).

Sholes, Jerry. *Give Me That Prime-Time Religion* (New York: Hawthorne Books, 1979).

Shriver, George H. *American Religious Heretics* (Nashville: Abingdon, 1966).

Southey, Robert. *The Life of Wesley: and the Rise and Progress of Methodism* (London: Bell and Daldy, 1864).

Stewart, John T. *The Deacon Wore Spats: Profiles from America's Changing Religious Scene* (New York: Holt, Reinhardt, and Winston, 1956).

Strober, Gerald, and Tomczak, Ruth. *Jerry Falwell: A Flame for God* (Nashville: Thomas Nelson, 1979).

Suenens, Cardinal L.J. *Une Nouvelle Pentecote?* (Brussels: Desclee De Brouwer, 1974).

Suzuki, Shunryu. *Zen Mind, Beginner's Mind* (New York and Tokyo: Weatherbill, 1973).

Talbot, Peter. *The Jesus Movement* (New York: National Board of YMCAs, 1972).

Thomas, William. *Assessment of Mass Meetings as a Method of Evangelism* (Amsterdam: Rodopi N.V., 1977).

Toynbee, Arnold. *Civilization on Trial* (New York: Oxford, 1948).

Van Allen, Roger. *American Values and the Future of America* (Philadelphia: Fortress, 1978).

Van Dusen, Henry P., "Third Force in American Christendom." *Life*, June 9, 1958.

Verkuyl, Jan. *Inleiding in de Nieuwere Zandingswetenschep* (Kampen: J.H. Kok, 1976).

Wagner, C. Pete. *Latin American Theology: Radical or Evangelical? The Struggler for the Faith in a Young Church* (Grand Rapids: Eerdmans, 1970).

Weisberger, Bernard A. *They Gathered at the River—The Story of the Great Revivalist and their Impact Upon Religion in America* (Boston: Little Brown, 1958).

Wells, David F., and Woodbridge, John D., ed., *The Evangelicals: What They Believe, Who They Are, Where They Are Changing* (Nashville: Abingdon Press, 1975).

"What's Wrong with Born-Again Politics?" *Christian Century 97* (October 22, 1980): 1002-4.

Williams, J. Paul. *What Americans Believe and How They Worship* (New York: Harper and Row, 1969).

Williams, William Carlos. *In the American Grain* (New York: Morrow, 1925).

Wills, Gary. *The Kennedy Imprisonment: A Meditation on Power* (Boston: Little, Brown, 1982).

Wirt, Sherwood Eliot. *The Social Conscience of the Evangelical* (New York: Harper & Row, 1968).

Wood, Robert W. *Christ and the Homosexual* (New York: Vantage Press, Inc., 1960).

Woodward, Kenneth. "A One Million Dollar Habit." *Newsweek 98* (September 15, 1980): 35.

Wylie, Irvin G. *The Self-Made Man in America: The Myth of Rags to Riches* (New York: Free Press, 1954).

Zweier, Robert, and Smith, Richard. "Christian Politics and the New Right." *Christian Century 99* (October 8, 1980): 937-42.